high acclaim for

YOUR GARAGENOUS ZONE

"Bill West is an innovator. His creative, humorous, and user-friendly ideas about how to use the 'largest room in your house,'—the garage—make this book the most important operating manual in your home."

—Larry Kendall, MBA, Chairman
The Group, Inc. Real Estate

"*Your Garagenous Zone* is the most complete book ever written about the garage. If you are determined to take back your garage and actually park a car in it, this book helps you do just that...*and more*. You will never look at your garage the same way after reading it."

—Barry J. Izsak, 2003-2004 President
National Association of Professional Organizers

"Bill West hits the nail on the head. He tells us how to fix this classic American problem! This is a makeover guide we can all use. It has inspired me to get busy in my own garage!"

—Bill Warren, President, CEO
National Inspection Services
Author of *Time/Life's Fix-It-Yourself* series

"Bill West does a tremendous service by focusing our attention of having the garage be a serviceable contribution to the quality of life. I love the historical perspective on the garage and his commentary on the garage of the future stimulates the imagination."

— Michelle Passoff, Author
Lighten Up! Free Yourself from Clutter

"At last, here's a book that resonates with anyone who endures piles of clutter in the garage. *Your Garagenous Zone* breaks down old concepts about how Americans have used the garage for over 100 years. Bill West generates positive ideas about how you can get a functional garage."

—Marc A. Shuman, President
GarageTek® Inc.

"West, whose...book details how to declutter the garage, preaches the gospel of organization."

—Minneapolis Star Tribune

"Bill West gives you a fresh approach to tackling a problem area we usually try to hide in our homes—the cluttered garage. It's amazing how following his simplified plan inspires and motivates the reader to clean up other areas of life also! You actually experience a new peace and harmony about yourself with *Your Garagenous Zone.*"

—Debra Benton, Author
New York Times best seller, *How to Think Like a CEO*
and her recent book, *Executive Charisma*

"For too long the garage is regarded as the stepchild of the American home. Fortunately, Bill West in his ingenious book, *Your Garagenous Zone*, embraces the space and elevates its status as a vital and valuable part of any home. This book contains everything you need to know to convert your disaster into a "Garage-Mahal!"

—James Carey, Co-host
On the House with the Carey Bros.
Nationally syndicated home improvement radio show

"*Your Garagenous Zone* is well researched, easy to read, attractively illustrated, and quite useful. If you're ready to join the national trend to renovate and upgrade the garage, Bill West's book is a great place to start. I recommend it without reservation."

—Tom Wadsworth, Editor
Door & Access Systems Newsmagazine

"We discovered *Your Garagenous Zone* book late into our market research [about the demand for reinventing the garage]. And your book validated our research for the initial product line for the Gladiator™ GarageWorks."

— Todd Starr, Product Development Director
Whirlpool® Corporation

"Bill West identifies so many core principles and models basic to visuality in the workplace and applies them to the last hold-out for domestic improvement—the garage! What a wealth of useful resources and solutions he offers in this sharp, thorough, fun book. Who of us wouldn't want to change the garage into a space that makes sense? *Your Garagenous Zone* shows us how!"

—Gwendolyn Galsworth, Ph.D., Author
Visual Systems: Harnessing the Power of a Visual Workplace
and *Smart Simple Design*

YOUR GARAGENOUS ZONE

Innovative Ideas for the Garage

Bill West, CRS

FIRST EDITION

Edited by Joe Lewandowski

Paragon ■ Garage

COMPANY LTD

Fort Collins, Colorado

Paragon Garage Company, Ltd., Fort Collins 80525
©2004 by the Paragon Garage Company, Ltd.
13 12 11 10 09 08 07 06 05 04   1 2 3 4 5

ISBN (Pbk.): 0-9675875-0-6

Publisher's Cataloging-in-Publication

West, Bill, 1951-
    Your garagenous zone : innovative ideas for the
garage / Bill West ; edited by Joe Lewandowski ; - 1st ed.

p. cm.
LCCN 2003099508
ISBN 0-9675875-0-6

    1. Garages—Unites States.   I. Lewandowski, Joe
II. Title.

NA8348.W47 2004   728'.98
                    QBI33-1753

PRINTED IN THE UNITED STATES OF AMERICA!

∞The paper used in this publication meets the minimum requirements of the American
National Standard for Information Sciences—Permanence of Paper for Printed Library
Materials, ANSI Z 39.48-1992.

Dedication

To my wife, Beverly Donnelley, and our son, Taylor West,
who are my inspiration every day.

Cover design and book layout by Becky S. Asmussen, Image Graphics, Loveland, Colorado

Author photo by Cambon Studios

"Only in America do we leave cars worth thousands of dollars in the driveway and leave useless junk in the garage."

from **Only in America**

Contents

Preface

Innovative ideas surround each of us in daily life. Some ideas are major technological break-throughs; others add simplicity and convenience for living in the 21st century. Many of today's major corporations got their start in the humble garage. Ironically, innovative ideas have escaped organizing inside of the garage — until recently.

The garage exists as the final frontier in our homes to become 'civilized.' It is the largest, most underutilized, most abused, and most often ignored room in the home. And these days, many garages are getting bigger and not always better.

Home owners express their utter discontent with the clutter and complete disorganization that prompts feelings of resignation. I wrote this book for people who prefer to own a clean, functional, and organized garage. And I'll show how it gets done for the handy do-it-yourselfer, by calling a professional organizer, or by hiring a company to arrive at the house to outfit and furnish your garage in a day or two.

This is the only book for this new category in home improvement that outlines a strategy to accomplish the goal of transforming garage futility into garage utility. Use this book as a reference guide often to tackle various projects to restore your garage. You will also discover many products and services for the garage that can make life and the garage better than perhaps you ever dreamed possible. I have been developing organizing concepts based on the products for the garage that I have researched since I remodeled and organized my garage in 1998.

I hope this book will serve you as a source of inspiration and a resource for innovation in your garage. Yes, there is hope for your garage.

Bill West
Fort Collins, Colorado
March 8, 2004

Acknowledgments

Throughout my real estate career, I inform customers desiring to build a new home to be mentally prepared. I embellish the notion that there are "only 7,500 decisions to make when building a new home" to emphasize the point. 'Building' a book is much the same as building a home—I received lots of help.

Charles Tremendous Jones, a national speaker dripping with inspiration, remarked, "The person you are in five years is based on two things: the people you meet and the books you read." The people I have met over the years in this nascent business have inspired me to write this book. My sincere thanks to all of them.

My wife, *Beverly Donnelley,* was supportive of me the moment I suggested writing the first book and now this one. You're the greatest!

Marty Tjelmeland, my long-time friend, is a skilled carpenter who built my workbench, remodeled my garage, and provided some illustrations for this book.

Jay Behm, garage designer, provided drawings to be included in my first book and now this one. Much thanks.

Butch Sommermeyer offered his insights that expanded my thinking about the electrical systems in the garage.

Bill Warren, an author of many books and articles about home construction, stepped forward offering to review my work.

Gary Hendrickson, a nationally known Feng Shui expert and instructor, contributed his expertise to illustrate the benefits in the garage from this ancient Chinese practice.

Dawn Michele Evans, vice president and director of marketing for The Evans Group, shared her insights and resources.

Don Evans, Barry A. Berkus, Anton M. Dattilo are all great architects. They contributed their design ideas and shared their talents for this book.

My fraternity brothers from various chapters of The Fraternity of Alpha Kappa Lambda, namely, *Dean Butler, Vaughn Hysinger, Dr. Robert Crosier, Floyd DePalma, Herb Hinstorff, Dr. Lloyd Glawe,* and *Bruce Wyckoff* photographed some of the famous garages in my first book and now this one. Some of the garages were gone, but their efforts are appreciated. Thank you for your spirit of brotherhood. It is Affiliation Kindled for Life.

Sam Solt, a good friend, lent his insights which are beyond measure. His passion for garages continues to impress and inspire me.

Joe Lewandowski, my editor, provided me with efficient and incisive work. He was never lost for words.

Becky Asmussen, my book designer and layout specialist, has a great sense of style and color that are beyond measure. And she's a kind person.

All of my partners at my employment, *The Group, Inc. Real Estate* have been supportive. They are world-class Realtors® and great people.

Finally, *Joyce's Java* provided me with that jolt of java each morning. Foregoing my cup of Joe would surely have meant falling asleep on the computer keyboard. And that would have left a mark.

"Our garage is a mess.
Someday we'll organize the garage."

— Anonymous home owner

BOB'S STORY: an introduction

A typical Saturday morning in spring

Peering through the kitchen window from inside his home, Bob sees the sunlight brightly reflecting the morning dew as if diamonds had been sprinkled on his freshly-cut lawn. Bob prepares for the long day ahead by nibbling on dry toast as he pours his second cup of coffee. He contemplates nothing that can interfere with his planned activity on such a beautiful day. He is focused.

As he gulps the last of his coffee, he glances at his watch, shouts to his wife that he is leaving the house and exits to the room of gloom: the garage.

He instinctively presses the button to open the garage door. The metal curtain rises shedding light on the piles of clutter and stacks of debris that typically litter the garage floor. Bob negotiates his way around the family cars, high-steps over the lawnmower, and stutter-steps between the tall and narrow stacks of cardboard boxes, contents unknown, left over from the move to the new house last summer. He dances around the bicycles and lifts the weed whacker from his path. Then he kicks aside a few bundles of newspapers ready to be recycled. But he cannot find what he is looking for.

Bob glances at his watch. It's later than he thought. He two-steps around a home-improvement project in process, then approaches the sawdust-laden canvas cover. Using both hands, he deftly swipes the canvas cover into the air, and as the sawdust cascades over his clean attire, he spots the prize-his golf clubs.

The golf bag served as a refuge for spiders since last fall judging by the look of the dense netting of webs. Shaking his golf towel, Bob wipes away the webs and dusts off the sawdust from his clothes as best as he can. With golf clubs in tow, he retraces his path to the trunk of his car, narrowly avoiding a tumbling column of boxes falling from against the wall.

Golf clubs finally secured in the trunk of the car, Bob backs out of the driveway and heads down the street. Bob will discover later that spiders were not the only inhabitants in the golf bag. When he pulls out his golf shoes, he finds that a family of mice found them to be a good fit over the long winter.

Pressed for time, Bob presses the gas pedal to make up for the lost time as he maneuvers through the subdivision's streets. Not escaping his attention are the contents from various neighbors' garages piled high in driveways making way for the semi-annual hose flushing of garage floors.

Bob's neck muscles tighten with guilt. He remembers his wife requesting on more than one occasion that he clean out their garage. His procrastination is producing pangs of anxiety.

Arriving home later that afternoon from his double-bogey round of golf, Bob watches the garage door open. He is greeted with the painful sight of the disarray that he so hastily escaped from earlier.

He mutters to himself out loud, "There must be a better way than living with a landfill attached to the house."

"There must be a better way than living with a landfill attached to the house."

There *is* a better way if you are tired of wasting time looking for certain items in your grungy, grimy, and greasy garage. As one newspaper reporter who read this book wrote: "After buying my third tape measure in two weeks, I decided it was time I organized my garage." He did organize his garage based on the recommendations in this book. Misplacing two tape measures is the result of a culmination of events that occurred over months, perhaps years. After reading *Your Garagenous Zone®*, he recognized the benefits that a clean and organized garage can produce for the entire family.

Consider this suggestion as this book is being read: Suspend every belief, every idea, and every notion that occupies your mind about your garage. The bargain that I offer is the following: Maintain an open mind, and I will present logical ideas that will inspire, inform, and transform your attitude and in the process transcend garage futility into garage utility.

Since starting to sell real estate in 1977, I have seen thousands of garages. Home owners invariably lamented: "Our garage is a mess." And the refrain, "some day we'll get it organized."

Maintain an open mind, and I will present logical ideas that will inspire, inform, and transform your attitude and in the process transcend garage futility into garage utility.

The problem for home owners is that, until now, there has been no systematic approach to begin the daunting task of organizing the garage. With this book in hand, your *some day* is closer. You can reclaim garage space and create a multipurpose room suitable for the entire family.

You do not need to possess the rugged, do-it-yourself skills required for many home-improvement projects. There exist many options in the marketplace to help home owners achieve a fully finished and organized garage without pounding a nail or breaking one. Let your fingers do the walking instead of the caulking. Because if there is not a garage remodeling and organizing company near you, one will be established very soon. Take a look in the 'Garage Storage and Organizing' or similarly-named category in the yellow-page section of the telephone book for a service near you.

This book serves as a resource to home owners choosing to undertake a garage remodeling and organizing project. In addition to explaining design concepts, I discuss garage products that I have researched and used. This book is not a catalog from which products are sold. No promotional fees were received from the product makers appearing in this book. Your Garagenous Zone® is a repository of philosophy and a compendium of ideas, which will benefit you and your home.

Given that garage remodeling and organizing is a new concept in home improvement, I wrote a test-market edition of this book outlining objectives, my philosophy, and I also researched products. The test-market edition has been read by home owners in all 50 states, Canada, Puerto Rico, London and even Bangkok. Based on the feedback that I have received from readers, this new home-improvement concept is being firmly embraced.

"The entire project is finished and it looks wonderful. We love it! We followed your guide religiously and we're so glad we did. It's like we've added a whole new room to our house. We've been hanging out in there a lot! Thanks so much for everything." — **Caroline O., Lindon, Utah**

"Enclosed are pictures from our finished garage. I want you to know that your garage handbook was very helpful in the design and execution of the project. I regret not taking "before" pictures so you could see the contrast. It was pretty ugly... We are very pleased with the result." — **Bill D., Vienna, Virginia**

"Your book has a lot of helpful and useful information. Your book has really motivated us to organize not only the garage, but the entire house. Thanks again!" — **Kathy K., Champaign, Illinois**

WEST'S LAWS OF CLUTTER

West's First Law of Clutter:
Void of organizational systems, clutter tends to expand over time in direct proportion to the volume of space in any given, finite environment.

West's Second Law of Clutter:
Every object in a collection of disarray in any given space tends to remain in that state until an external force is applied to it.

West's Third Law of Clutter:
For every action of not putting an object in its place after using it, there is an opposite and undesirable reaction when attempting to locate and use that object again resulting in time wasted looking for it.

RESOLVING THE LANDFILL MENTALITY IN THE GARAGE

> **WARNING:** This book could cause marital strife in the event that one spouse desires to have a clean, functional, and organized garage, and the spouse-in-denial prefers the garage to remain in its constant state of disarray. The author cannot be responsible for marital discontent, but he offers some techniques for conflict resolution.

While I have received lots of positive feedback, from time to time, I would hear from someone, who, half jokingly, would say: "You have created a rift in our marriage. My wife (or my husband) wants to organize our garage, and I don't!" Why would anyone want to have a greasy, grimy, grungy garage? But I accepted the idea that conflicts arise between spouses on any number of topics especially when the topic is a home remodeling project!

As luck would have it, I received a telephone call from Polly Zeleny, a local interior designer and author of *Creating Your Life Space*. She wanted to arrange some time with me to explain what her book was about. I agreed.

When Polly arrived at my office for our appointment, I was intrigued by her ideas. *Creating Your Life Space* describes holistic ways to create a home environment that reflects the person you are *and* how you relate to others in creating that home environment. Her 20-question "Life Traits Quiz" reveals the characteristics and the strategies that each of us employ in establishing our preferences in a home environment.

This self-scoring quiz provides insight into the preferences of a partner. Polly's book is based, in part, on the Swiss psychologist Carl G. Jung's four personality types theory, which is a systematic approach to discovering certain, basic characteristics that we all possess.

My wife and I took the quiz and the results were amazing to us. By understanding what is important to each of us, we work to accommodate and support the type of home environment that we create together. For example, my wife possesses dominant traits that are

creative, dynamic, and rarely limits herself or her possibilities, which translates into her unlimited bravery for bold colors for some areas of the interior in our home. On the other hand, my dominant traits are private, precise, and I enjoy order and the outcome of a process. She understands my desire to create and maintain order in the household, and I realize that a vibrant color that I would never dare to consider can be integrated with some interior design techniques and furniture.

Polly has broken the code of how people think, visualize, feel, and relate to one another about their home environment. By understanding this code, couples will avoid strife and misunderstandings when building a new home, undertaking a remodeling project, or, yes, reaching a decision about remodeling and organizing a garage.

To obtain Polly Zeleny's book, *Creating Your Life Space,* visit her website at www.Concept360.com, or get it at Barnes & Noble bookstores.

Here is another idea to resolve conflict: I created a game to help the spouse-in-denial better understand the importance of creating a clean and organized garage.

Garage scavenger hunt

RULES:

1. The spouse desiring a clean and organized garage obtains the willingness and commitment from the spouse-in-denial to play the game.

2. The spouse-in-denial agrees to take whatever time is needed to finish the game.

3. The spouse desirous of the organized garage makes a list of *five* known objects that are currently located in the garage.

4. The game may require minutes, hours, or days, but it is critical to know the amount of time spent looking for these objects. The spouse-in-denial must maintain a time log.

5. The spouse-in-denial searches for the five objects.

If all of the objects are located in a matter of a few minutes, the spouse-in-denial may gloat. But often it is the case that the other spouse cannot find them.

Reversing the roles with a new list can validate the test, but an earnest effort must be applied to locate the objects in the new list. More than likely, the spouse-in-denial will spend far more time than desired looking for all five objects. But the time log tells the tale: If more than a minute is expended searching for each object, time is being wasted. Even one minute is actually a generous allotment. In a garage that is systematically organized, items can be found in seconds. When time is squandered, life is squandered. It's all a choice.

The popular song "Looking for Love in all the Wrong Places" sung by Johnny Lee, could be modified slightly to reflect "Looking for *Stuff* in all the Wrong Places." Country Western song titles possess a knack for telling a story, which renders the lyrics needless. Since the title expresses a tone of lament, try on these titles:

"I Thought I Left My Cluttered Life Behind Until
I Took a Cluttered Woman to be Mine"

"My House is all cluttered, and My Husband's a Mess"

"I Ain't Married to Martha Stewart, but who'd want a
Husband Named Martha Anyway?"

A little humor is a good companion wherever you go even when you remodel and organize your garage.

Your Garagenous Zone
Innovative Ideas
for the
Garage

1. When in doubt, throw it out

2. Categorize before you organize

3. Organize to visualize:
   If you can see it, you can find it

4. If it's on the floor, it's time to store

5. Lateral thinking maximizes vertical storage

6. Keep it neat, treat the concrete

7. Put it away and the garage will stay
   that way—ORGANIZED

8. Your ride belongs inside!

9. Don't be hasty. Practice safety

THE GARAGENOUS ZONE® MODEL:
Nine objectives for a functional
& organized garage

By understanding the nine objectives in the creation of a functional and organized garage, you can look at the garage with a new perspective and unlock fresh ideas. These nine objectives work together supporting one another for the same outcome much like the nine players on a baseball team work in concert to win the game.

Most of the time, our thinking is restricted "inside the box." Sometimes thinking outside of the box requires grabbing hold of that box, shaking it, dumping out the contents, and creating something new inside. Now is the time to reinvent the Great American Garage.

This exercise illustrates thinking outside the box. Connect the numbers below using *only four* straight lines. *Keep the pen on paper and don't retrace over any lines.* Can you do the task? The following page has the solution.

1	2	3
4	5	6
7	8	9

See how an innovative approach changes the perspective and the outcome?

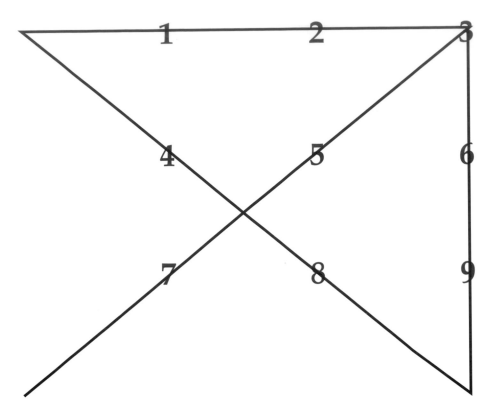

Objective nine promotes garage safety. Being the final objective in no way suggests that it is the least important. Calling attention to the safety objective here is sounding an alert. For a garage to be completely functional, it is required to be safe.

1. When in doubt, throw it out

Take an inventory of what is in the garage to determine what is excess. Excess pertains to objects that provide little or no value to the quality of life in your home environment.

When deciding what possessions to keep, ask and answer, this question: "How does this item add value to our lives?" All of us, at one time or another, allow stuff to cling to us like some invisible, magnetic force. "But I might need this some day," is the typical rationale when pondering whether to keep, for example, a worn-out bristle brush. Only by taking inventory will you rediscover what you "might need some day." Imagine your heirs rifling through your possessions after you are dead. Can you imagine them saying, "What on earth did she keep this for?"

So, take a deep breath, decide what needs to be sold, given to charity, or

Living in and with clutter blocks energy. When you are energized, it is far easier to get organized.

1-800-GOT-JUNK? removes the clutter and excess that you've wanted to eliminate for years.

---

thrown away. Place items that are to be sold in a box. Place items to be given to charity in another box; and trash the rest. Taking action to remove items that clutter our lives is a freeing experience. I guarantee you will experience a surge of positive energy and a sense of resolve when you finally take action. Living in and with clutter blocks energy. When you are energized it is far easier to get organized.

You're not alone if paralysis immobilizes your forward progress to remove the clutter in your life. Before you consider therapy, call the fine folks at 1-800-GOT-JUNK? They specialize in what you despise—junk. Your prison is their passion.

2. Categorize before you organize

Getting organized is more than just placing objects on a newly-installed shelf. Think in categories to provide the basis for an organizing scheme.

The best way to understand this objective is to study how a kitchen is designed. Can you imagine a kitchen without cabinets, counter space or drawers? Just think of the chaos and clutter! Fortunately, kitchens are well designed. But because design is not considered for the garage space, it becomes little more than a dumpster or storage unit attached to the house.

A well-designed kitchen includes a work triangle as the premise for its layout. The sink is in close proximity to the refrigerator for quick retrieval of food to be prepared. Then the oven or range top is near the sink for easy placement for the food to be cooked. Think of the sink, refrigerator, and stove as the points of the work triangle. While food is cooking, other dishes can be prepared, but a close eye can be kept on what is on the stove.

Remember, if it's easy for the mind, it's easy for you to find.

The amount of sporting equipment can be overwhelming, but categorizing equipment in a cabinet eliminates clutter and saves time.

Ingredients used routinely are kept in a cabinet or pantry close by. Utensils, plates, cups, and pans are located strategically in cabinets or drawers for efficiency. The Sunday-best China, large bowls, casserole dishes, etc. are stored in cabinets that are not as close because those items are not used everyday.

Now, think of your garage. By establishing categories for your stuff, you can imagine how garage space can be utilized to make items accessible. Remember, if it's easy for the mind, it's easy for you to find.

Here are some garage categories:

- **Lawn and garden**
- **Automotive**
- **Hardware supplies**
- **Sporting equipment**
- **Tools**
- **Shoes/boots**
- **Staple food items**
- **Kid's toys**
- **Camping equipment**

Arranging the garage in categories enables any family member to know where to look for anything at any time!

For example, if a family stores a lot of food in the garage, it is best to locate the pantry, freezer, or refrigerator near the door that leads into the house. Buy an upright freezer because it requires less floor space and it is safer than the chest type.

Some families participate in so many sports that sorting within this category is necessary for a variety of equipment. One solution: Each family member could have their own locker(s).

If you want a functional garage but lack the inclination to delve into any project that requires organizing skills, I have included a Geographical Directory of the National Association of Professional Organizers. Members can help anyone get their garage organized. They can also assist you in other areas of the home or workplace. The directory is on page 163.

3. Organize to visualize: If you can see it, you can find it

Finding an object in the garage is often as difficult as going into a darkened, unfamiliar room to find a specific object. Americans waste a lot of time looking for things especially in the garage. The typical garage is a black hole into which objects disappear. Then on moving day they suddenly reappear.

Creating a flexible, visually organized system enables you to locate an object with ease and efficiency. Even when items are stored in closed cabinets, knowing the category of the items prompts quick recognition about where those objects are located.

Professional organizer Kevin Hall from San Diego, California, suggests labeling everything. Place plastic pockets on the outside of cabinet doors and insert a label to identify the category and contents. This tip works well for storage boxes that are stored in open shelving. When the contents change in the cabinet or storage box, the label can be easily switched. Mr.

The typical garage is a black hole into which objects disappear. Then on moving day they suddenly reappear.

Hall explains the associated benefit of this labeling technique: "The uniformity creates a calming effect and is void of visual graffiti."

Storage needs change. That is why it is important to incorporate a flexible organizing system into any well-designed garage scheme. That is particularly important for the walls. Mounting pegs, racks, or hooks eliminate flexibility in how that space is used—not to mention pock marks they make.

4. If it's on the floor, it's time to store

The garage floor serves as the catch-all location by default when there appears to be no other place to store stuff. Over time, these objects collectively transform into clutter eventually edging out automobiles of their rightful place in the garage. One reason the cluttered garage is the room to avoid is due to the vast number of obstacles 'stored' on the floor. It is a battleground for fighting through the barriers for easy movement.

Until now, using the floor as a 'shelf' is justifiable because many garages have not possessed organizing systems as part of garage design. When I clean my garage, the only items stored on the floor are our son's wagon and bicycle, treadmill, tool chest, and recycle bin. The dog bed and food dish are easily set aside. That's it. Other items formerly relegated to the garage floor, now have specific places to be stored. The time to mop the garage floor is measured in minutes, not in hours, as are usually required to clean a typical garage.

Floor clutter invites rodents.

Clearing the floor maximizes space for human movement, for parking the car, and eliminates safety hazards. The visible results produce a positive feeling that garage space can be more than just a jungle of junk.

Prior to remodeling and organizing my garage in 1998, rodents sought refuge in the garage especially beginning in early fall. Our house is near a golf course and the back is surrounded by 56 acres of open space, both are havens for all kinds of critters.

Since the completion of the garage project, no evidence of rodents exists. I cannot guarantee similar results in other well-organized garages, but without floor clutter, where are they to hide?

Clearing the floor maximizes space for human movement, for parking the car, and eliminates safety hazards. The visible results produce a positive feeling that garage space can be more than just a jungle of junk.

5. Lateral thinking maximizes vertical storage

Most homes include a one or two-car garage. Storage space is limited. One perspective could lead one to say, "If I had a three-car garage, I could accomplish all of this storage and organizing too." But consider the same person saying this: "Since I have a two-car garage, these storage and organizing ideas become more valuable to me."

The existing garage remains, but possibilities expand with some creative thinking. For example, walls, the ceiling, support posts, rafters, and soffits develop storage previously unimagined.

An example of lateral thinking: support posts in the garage create organizing space.

Garages in newer homes have high ceilings. One home owner in Florida created a loft in the garage that he uses to store car parts. He converted dead space into usable space. His wife is pleased, too. She does not have to negotiate around greasy car parts on the way to her car.

Garage design, creating storage, achieving a clean and organized garage provides many benefits to the home owner. Creating a functional garage can become a very engaging experience.

6. Keep it neat, treat the concrete

Raw, exposed concrete absorbs motor fluids and dirt creating an unsightly mess. That dirt and grime also is tracked into the house. Concrete is porous making it difficult to clean. Keeping it clean is an exercise in futility.

Floor paint often blisters, flakes, and degrades rapidly especially when the floor is confronted with hot, street-driven tires. Home owners experiencing this menace to their near-new, painted floor can only grimace. I have experienced similar results in homes previously owned. Many products are substandard.

Fortunately, advanced products for the garage floor are available. Today's coatings and rubberized flooring material are easy to clean and maintain.

7. Put it away and the garage will stay that way—ORGANIZED

An organized, functional space produces efficiency. In a well-organized garage, a tool or garden implement that is not returned to its prescribed location disrupts the system. The misplaced implement requires someone's time to look for and retrieve it.

All humans have tendencies to become distracted and forgetful from time to time. Making an effort to return items is much better than allowing things to pile up. In the organized garage, there is a system that works at least, most of the time. Attempting to create a species of efficiency experts is of no interest to most of us. What we all hope for is improvement, which is worthy of our time in all of life's endeavors.

Attempting to create a species of efficiency experts is of no interest to most of us. What we all hope for is improvement, which is worthy of our time in all of life's endeavors.

8. Your ride belongs inside!

It may seem obvious that the primary purpose of a garage is to park your car. But many garages in America now serve as storage units for stuff. The U. S. Department of Energy discovered that home owners with at *least* a three-car garage usually parked only one or *none* of their cars in the garage!

Clearing the streetscape with fewer cars is a worthy goal. Kept inside, the car cannot be vandalized; entering the home from a closed garage promotes personal safety. Be kind to your car and park it in the garage.

9. Don't be hasty. Practice safety

While many garages are hazard zones, *The Garagenous Zone*® model supports safety in each objective. Because the garage can accommodate multiple activities, it should be a safe environment for all family members. Take to heart the following suggestions, and take time to practice safety in the garage:

- Eliminate floor clutter to avoid tripping. Keep the floor clean.
- Don't store flammable materials in glass containers.
- Store flammable materials in metal containers that meet Underwriters Laboratory safety standards.
- Avoid use of extension cords which create a fire hazard. A fire caused by a faulty extension cord could void your insurance contract in the event of a claim.
- Place power tools, extension cords, rope, or twine in a secure or high cabinet safely away from little hands.
- Lock gasoline, paint thinner, antifreeze, chemicals, pesticides, and solvents in a cabinet, and be sure each is in its original container with label.
- All containers should include child-resistant caps.
- All electrical outlets should be on a GFI (Ground Fault Interrupter) circuit.
- Some garages have a curb, step-up level, or landing area separating the parking area from the entrance to the house. Apply a three-inch strip of yellow paint on the top and front face of the step to serve as a visual warning.
- Install a covering or shade over the window to a service door for security. A service door leads from the garage to the back or side yards.
- Install a motion detector that activates a light on the outside near the service door.
- Install a deadbolt on the service door.

- Wear safety glasses while working on a project, and make sure they are easy to find.

- Place a fire extinguisher in an accessible area in the garage. The extinguisher should be capable of putting out all three types of fires—combustible solids, flammable liquids, and electrical fires. Next to the fire extinguisher, place a first-aid kit and know how to use it.

- Install a cordless phone in the garage.

- The Consumer Products Safety Commission recommends performing safety checks on the garage door.

- Replace garage doors installed before 1982. Many old doors do not work properly because of age, installation, or lack of maintenance.

- The Consumer Products Safety Commission requires all electric door openers to include an automatic reverse mechanism. Replace automatic door openers that do not have this safety feature.

- Invest in a garage door monitor. The monitor is placed in a visible location in the home and indicates if the garage door is open. A county sheriff's department reported 100 burglaries during a year in one neighborhood. The deputy said that closing the garage doors would reduce thievery by 85% to 90%. An open garage door is an invitation for thieves to enter the home.

- Teach all family members about garage safety.

REINVENTING THE GARAGE:
How to create the
Garagenous Zone® model

The nine objectives express the foundation for creating a functional and organized garage. This section shows how to do it from floor to ceiling and wall to wall.

Knowing 'how much' before 'how to' is the first question most home owners ask before undertaking a remodeling project. The cost to finish a garage using a contractor is approximately $10-$14 per square foot based on the ideas in this section. Results vary by region based on labor and material costs. The square-foot cost is used because it is the accepted method for understanding the overall cost of a building or remodeling project.

By comparison, the cost to build a basic home with a contractor in many parts of the country is about $100 per square foot excluding the land cost and much more per square foot in other regions of the country. To professionally finish a basement costs approximately $26 to $30 a square foot. But these costs can vary widely based on quality of finish.

Before getting started, check with your local building department to determine if a permit is required to remodel and organize the garage. A municipal building inspector in one jurisdiction indicates no need to obtain a building permit. A permit will be required for electrical and plumbing work and for adding built-in heating systems. If the garage is converted to living space, then most municipalities require a building permit. The work to remodel and organize the garage is considered cosmetic by most cities.

When there is no building permit, the investment to remodel and organize the garage does not affect the assessed valuation for the house. The result for your property tax is neutral. There may be some cities with rigorous building permit requirements.

A note of caution: Be careful if you plan interior demolition in the garage. Asbestos insulation or asbestos material that wraps around heating ducts can be a hazard, especially in older homes. So before interior demolition occurs, know the risks for any airborne material that can affect the respiratory system.

If you are doing the work in your garage, be sure to wear a respirator and safety glasses.

The cost for products is excluded because of varied pricing structures for some products throughout the country and promotional offers that may occur from time to time.

The workbench: garage furniture

The workbench is the focal point for any garage. Most activity in the garage centers on the workbench. The workbench can be used as the family project center for activities in the garage. Home fix-up projects, science fair experiments, making crafts, and other activities can be completed on the workbench.

Elevating the workbench eliminates lower back strain while working on a project.

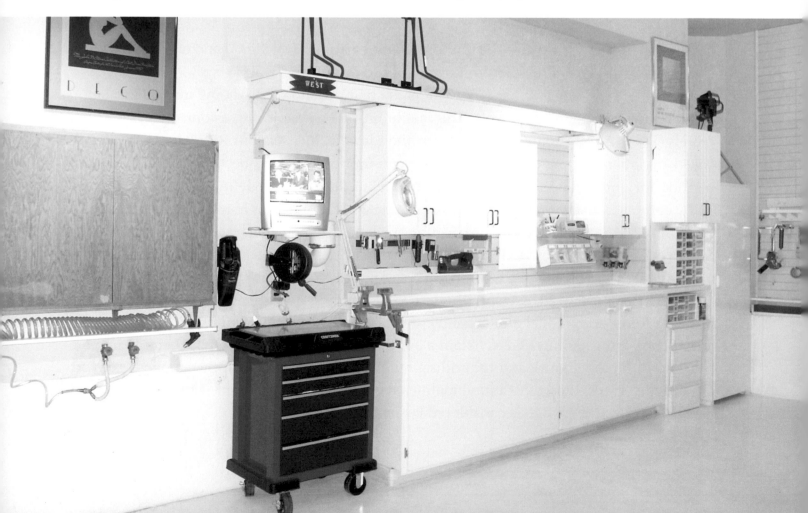

Automotive enthusiasts or serious wood workers might exclaim, "Hey, wait a minute, this is my space!" Nothing is absolute. The ideas set forth here suggest new possibilities for the garage and take nothing away from anyone. Garages continue to be used for a specific activity by one person in some households. And even when the garage is the sole domain used by one member of the family, many ideas presented here can facilitate creating organized space that is more functional and more enjoyable.

Many workbenches are constructed 30" to 36" tall. This presents a problem for many people because that is too low, and the lower height requires stooping which places strain on the lower back. Building the workbench 40" to 42" tall solves this nagging problem for many. There is no *perfect* workbench height because for a family it becomes impractical to suggest one size fits all.

The higher workbench adds a big benefit: Larger items such as the wet/dry vacuum or a trash receptacle can be stored beneath the workbench.

The size of your garage space usually dictates how long the workbench can be. It is recommended to make it as long as practical. It is far easier to work on a bench surface that is six-feet or eight-feet long than on a four-foot-long workbench.

Another benefit a longer workbench provides is the additional space on the wall above the work surface. Tools that are used frequently are easier to retrieve when stored above the work surface.

This illustration shows all the materials necessary to build a workbench.

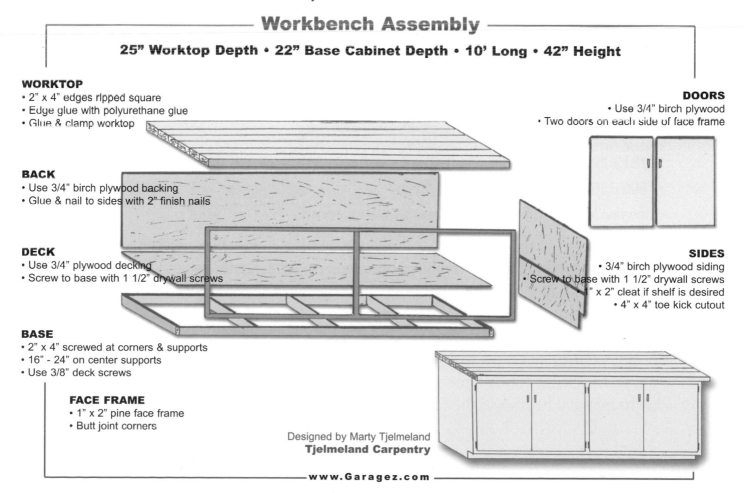

Workbench Assembly

25" Worktop Depth • 22" Base Cabinet Depth • 10' Long • 42" Height

WORKTOP
• 2" x 4" edges ripped square
• Edge glue with polyurethane glue
• Glue & clamp worktop

BACK
• Use 3/4" birch plywood backing
• Glue & nail to sides with 2" finish nails

DECK
• Use 3/4" plywood decking
• Screw to base with 1 1/2" drywall screws

BASE
• 2" x 4" screwed at corners & supports
• 16" - 24" on center supports
• Use 3/8" deck screws

FACE FRAME
• 1" x 2" pine face frame
• Butt joint corners

DOORS
• Use 3/4" birch plywood
• Two doors on each side of face frame

SIDES
• 3/4" birch plywood siding
• Screw to base with 1 1/2" drywall screws
• 1" x 2" cleat if shelf is desired
• 4" x 4" toe kick cutout

Designed by Marty Tjelmeland
Tjelmeland Carpentry

Leave one end of the workbench open and unobstructed. Some designs place cabinets or pantries on both ends of the workbench. This restricts activities that can be accomplished on the workbench.

Build the work surface of the workbench with at least a 3" overhang on the sides and 2 1/2" overhang on the front. This allows for vises and clamping devices to attach with ease. The top should be at least 1 1/2" thick to provide a sturdy work area. The surface should be no deeper than 25". A bench deeper than 25" requires a longer and more difficult stretch for most people.

The base of the workbench should include a 4" toe kick. In other words, make sure there is at least 4" of space beneath the workbench so you can stand against it while working on a project.

Check out the workbench assembly on the previous page to see how each section of a workbench can be put together. The design for any workbench should be sturdy enough to take on any rugged punishment from a variety of projects.

The walls: storage & organizing solutions

Hammering a few nails on the garage wall to hang a shovel and broom or to mount a shelf represents the old solution for storing and organizing. Fortunately, new products meet the demands for the 'over-stuffed' society. The following companies specialize in cabinets and wall organizing systems. Their products organize and maximize functionality.

GARAGE CABINETS

MITCHELL Garage Cabinet Systems

1615 North Country Club Road, Suite A, Stillwater, OK 74075

800.350.6427/Office 405.707.7166

www.MitchellGarageCabinetSystems.com

Brothers Don and Mike Mitchell are co-founders of this innovative company. Don's passion is reflected by making continuous improvements in designing garage cabinets. Don helped start the company in 2002 after leaving another leading cabinet maker where he was the driving force in design and manufacturing. Don is also the national sales and marketing manager. Mike is in charge of operations.

I researched the market for two years looking for cabinets. Particle board construction, I thought, seemed to be a compromise in quality. But I was incorrect. The furniture-grade particle board material he uses in the box frame of the cabinet helped change my attitude. Not all particle board is created equal. The frame is made with 3/4" particle board; three, dovetailed shelves provide rigidity.

The doors are made with 5/8" furniture-grade medium density fiberboard (MDF) and attach to the cabinet with three-way, adjustable Euro-style hinges.

The Steel-Rail Support System™ amplifies the strength of the cabinets. The rails enable the cabinets to be installed above the floor at any desired height. Angled notches on the back sides of the cabinet frame enable the steel rail to

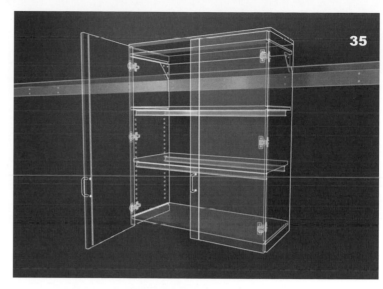

This illustration of **Mitchell Garage Cabinet Systems** shows the level of design innovation.

receive the cabinet flush against the wall. The height of the steel rail determines the location for each cabinet. Another benefit of elevated cabinets and pantry-style cabinets is easy floor cleaning. And there's no moisture absorption or wicking when the cabinets are elevated above the floor. This keeps pesky insects and rodents away too!

Installing cabinets on the wall is beneficial. All garage floors slope several inches toward the garage doors for drainage. Because floors are uneven by design, it is necessary to square each floor-mounted cabinet. Soil moves beneath concrete. Cabinets setting on the garage floor can shift out of square over time creating problems with closing doors properly as a result of pronounced floor movement.

Cabinets are available in sizes ranging from 18" to 84" in height. Cabinet depths range from 12" to 30", and widths are 12" to 48". The variety of cabinet options offers flexibility in configuring a customized layout. Many cabinets are designed for special uses such as storing brooms, fishing rods/skis, or golf clubs.

The **Steel-Rail Support System**™ is the backbone behind Mitchell Garage Cabinets.

M-BARS™ are steel inserts on which shelves are placed assuring no sagging over time.

Mount cabinets on the walls to meet current and future storage needs. You'll soon discover the pleasure of an organized garage.

Melamine cabinets by **MITCHELL** are available in white and grey stock colors.

The 72" pantry-style cabinets are available in depths of 12", 16" and 24". Pantry-style cabinets widths are 12", 24" and 36".

The workbench module is 31" high. But with leg extensions the height can increase to 40". These modules allow the length of the work surface to increase by 1', 2', or 3' increments beyond the standard workbench of 48" or 72". The work surface depths are 12", 16", 24" or 30". The finished work surface height varies depending on how high cabinets are mounted off the floor with leg extensions.

The workbench configurations provide numerous options for bins and drawers beneath the work bench surface. All workbench modules are pre-drilled to accommodate the flexibility for installing drawers and bins.

Other features include adjustable shelving come with most cabinets; cabinets are paintable providing the home owner color choices; cabinets can be sealed with an oil-based polyurethane which darkens the cabinet finish, or with a water-based polyurethane that maintains original cabinet color without streaking; and the load factor for cabinets is 300 pounds.

If you engage in water sports or fishing or live in regions with high humidity you might choose Mitchell Cabinets made with moisture-resistant Medex. The material, however, costs twice as much as standard grade cabinet material.

Mitchell Series 2 (MS2) is another line of melamine cabinets for the company. Standard colors are white and gray, which promote a brighter garage environment. Custom colors are available, but order delivery can be delayed. Not all cabinet sizes are available in the Melamine line.

Mitchell Garage Cabinet Systems has invested in state-of-the art manufacturing to provide home owners plenty of choices. As company founder Don Mitchell states, "Whatever the customer wants, we are going to supply it."

The company is represented nationally through independent dealers who provide no-cost estimates complete with layout and design. If there is no dealer located in your area, Mitchell Garage Cabinet Systems will ship direct complete with installation instructions.

SLIDE-LOK Garage & Storage Cabinets

503 West 3rd Avenue, Mesa, AZ 85210
800.835.1759
www.Slide-Lok.com

Slide-Lok Garage & Storage Cabinets company is employee-owned and started operations in 2002. It is a division of Bass Cabinets that has been in business since 1976. Bass Cabinets primarily manufactures and installs cabinetry in apartment complexes and condominium developments in the western U. S.

A distinguishing feature is the appearance of the cabinets. In fact, the material is plywood with a thermofuse finish. It looks and feels like natural maple or white-washed oak.

The ease of assembly is intuitive. While doing research on these cabinets, I took the parts from the shipping box and assembled the cabinet without reading the instructions.

The main body construction is 1/2" plywood, medium density fiberboard for shelving, and the face frames are made with 3/4" plywood. The doors are made with medium density fiberboard that uses the thermofuse process to obtain the same natural wood finish as the rest of the cabinet.

The cabinets feature 3/4" finished construction-grade adjustable shelves. The six-way adjustable, European hinges are easily concealed when the cabinet doors are closed.

Another distinguishing characteristic is the adjustable legs. Each leg adjusts from 3" to 6" inches. A 2"-leg extension also is available. The adjustable legs can compensate for the slope in the garage floor. The load

The thermofuse finish provides the look and feel of natural maple or white-washed oak.

factor is 775 pounds for a floor-mounted cabinet. The weight factor is important because these cabinets are stackable.

Director of National Sales Gary Smith explains that the modular design allows for a multitude of cabinet configurations. As storage needs change, more cabinets can be added.

Bill Miller, a distributor from South Lyon, Michigan emphasizes innovation when describing the Slide-Lok cabinets. "The patented dovetailed assembly system adds strength to each cabinet making assembly quick and easy," according to Mr. Miller.

Cabinet heights range from 24" to 48". Widths range 18" to 34". And depths range 16" to 24" for most cabinets. One wall cabinet is available with a 12" depth. The pantry is 24" x 68" with depths either 16" or 24".

Cabinets with 16" depths can be affixed when the wall organizer system StoreWALL™ is used (See StoreWALL™ below).

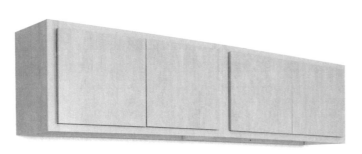

The StoreWALL™ hanging bracket is placed in a groove on the wall organizer. The bolt in the bracket extends through the back of the cabinet where it is secured with a nut and lock washer on the wall. Cabinets with greater depths cannot be affixed to the wall using this bracket.

Slide-Lok dealers in your area can be found on the company website at www.Slide-Lok.com. Dealers can help design the layout with the home owner and assemble cabinets. Or you can purchase and assemble the cabinets from the company website, Jack's

All cabinets include concealed
European hinges.

Cabinets can include easy-glide, roll-out
drawers for organizing

Design Center. You can create a custom design and layout online to meet specifications for your garage.

Cabinets can be purchased directly from the factory if no dealers are available in your area. An instructional CD is available with each order to aid in assembling the cabinets.

Slide-Lok adopts the garage cabinet construction developed from its parent company which makes residential cabinets. Some customers have commented that they would "love to have the garage cabinets in their house."

WALL ORGANIZING SYSTEMS

StoreWALL™ LLC

1699 North Astor, Milwaukee, WI 53202
(866) 889-2502/Office (414) 224-0878
www.Storewall.com

The only product this company manufactures is the StoreWALL™ organizing system. Before specializing, the company enjoyed a long history of producing a variety of extruded plastic products for other companies. The developed technology and expertise provided the unique capability to launch StoreWALL™ in 1997. With laser-beam focus, StoreWALL™ concentrates on delivering a product that is the standard in the industry.

Each panel is made with horizontal grooves to insert various accessories for hanging household objects and satisfying a wide variety of storage options. The panel sections can be combined to any length or height when installed. For cutting or drilling, use standard wood working tools. Use StoreWALL™ like any pre-finished material. Completing entire walls in the garage with StoreWALL™ provides flexible organizing for long-handled tools or

Attractive and durable **StoreWALL**™ Heavy Duty will help transform any garage into a showplace with emphasis on functionality.

---

brooms, sporting gear, folding chairs, and many other household items. The appearance of StoreWALL™ with the entire wall organizer installed provides a finished look similar to what you have in any room of your house.

The durability, strength, and a variety of attractive colors make StoreWALL™ ideal for the garage. The more I think about the possibilities, this product can be used in the laundry room, home office, basement store room, walk-in pantries, closets, and where open storage is needed.

Typically, StoreWALL™ is delivered in cartons that contain eight-foot lengths and four sections. Each section is 15". A carton provides 40 square feet of storage material.

StoreWALL™ has three installation methods that vary in load capacity depending on the installer's skill.

• **Screw installation**: This method produces high-load capacity with relatively low installation skills required. StoreWALL™ includes color-coordinated screws in 1-5/8" and 2-1/4" lengths that can be installed on wood or metal studs over existing drywall. Zinc plated and rust resistant, these screws require no pre-drilling or countersinking. The more screws used produces a greater load capability.

• **Adhesive installation**: Use only polyurethane adhesives because they create a stronger bond than conventional construction panel adhesives. Consider using a power brad nailer to fasten the panels while the adhesive sets usually in 24 hours. Adopting this method of installation should be considered permanent and requires professional tools.

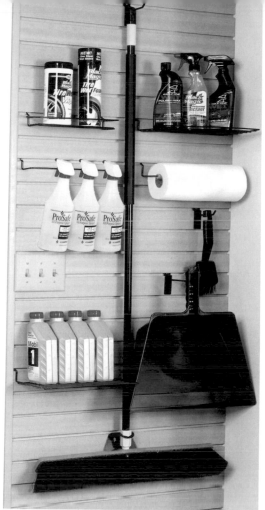

- **HangUp™ installation**: Precision and skill are required when employing this method, which provides for a moderate load capability but sufficiently high enough for most garages. There are no visible fasteners because the HangUps grip the panel from the back. A template assures accuracy. After the HangUps are attached to the wall, each panel can be installed.

For more detailed information, refer to the StoreWALL™ *Installation Tips manual.*

StoreWALL™ sets the standard for garage accessories because it is compatible with slat wall accessories used for store displays. There are distributors located virtually throughout the country selling slat wall accessories such as shelf brackets, hooks, racks, and baskets. Other companies such as Schulte, Racor, and The Accessories Group design accessories for home use that are compatible with StoreWALL™.

Kids know where to find toys and they know where to return them.

Cabinets can be installed on StoreWALL™. There are cabinets designed for StoreWALL™, and there are brackets that can be used on the back of standard cabinets.

StoreWALL™ comes in three designer colors and two authentic wood grains, which are solid core. Custom colors are available upon request.

- **Global Pine** - looks and feels like light maple or birch
- **Rustic Cedar** - similar to a medium-toned oak
- **Weathered Grey** - medium-grey tone with subtle grain appearance
- **Dover White** - warm off-white
- **Brite White** - a true designer white

StoreWALL™ is waterproof and weatherproof. This feature adds versatility for outdoor use in carports. I am planning to use StoreWALL™ on a wall over a potting bench. The walls in my garden shed are installed with StoreWALL™. Tools and implements are stored on the walls, so they're easy to find. Even the wheelbarrow is stored on the wall and out of the way.

StoreWALL™ can be found through its network of independent dealers.

StoreWALL™ Heavy Duty can tackle wall storage for every member of the family.

StoreWALL™ is waterproof and weatherproof

Displawall® by Marlite

202 Harger Street
P. O. Box 250,
Dover, OH 44622
Office 330.343.6621   www.Displawall.com

Walk into virtually any retail store and you'll see this type of product used to display merchandise.

Displawall® is manufactured in 4' x 8' panels. Material used is 3/4" medium density fiberboard. Each panel weighs about 70 pounds. Installation requires at least two people. The grooved panels accommodate only accessories made by Marlite. The finish is a modified melamine enamel topcoat that is baked on to the surface to achieve durability.

When installed according to manufacturer's instructions, Displawall® panels support approximately 36 pounds per bracket at 6" from the panel face. Support testing is based on random samples and may not be indicative of individual results, according to Marlite literature. Marlite produces a variety of solid color, patterns, and wood-grain like finishes from which to choose.

Standard panels include standard factory-painted grooves that harmonize with the standard panel surface. ColorSnaps™ are solid vinyl inserts in 12 standard colors. Inserts snap into each groove after installation to conceal the fasteners. ColorSnaps™ create design flexibility apart from the standard panel because of the variety of color choices.

For the die-hard, do-it-yourself remodeler, paint-grade panels are available with a smooth surface. These panels are more economical. And the home owner can customize color and finish. Polyurethane is an acceptable finish too.

DISPLAWALL™ comes in 4' x 8' sheets made of medium density fiberboard.

Before you install Displawall® panels, be sure to read the company requirements: "Remove panels from the cartons and allow them to acclimatize to room conditions for 48 hours; stand up each panel to be installed separately; keep in a cool, dry environment not exceeding 70ºF; all exterior walls should include a vapor barrier to minimize warping." Note the heat factor and periods of high humidity can affect the product installed in the garage. I have had

Displawall® in my Colorado garage since 1998. Extreme weather conditions have not affected the product from my experience. Areas with high humidity could affect the product more severely.

Be sure to install panels high enough above the garage floor to avoid contact with moisture. The panels can be installed to studs in the garage. Some garage walls have drywall already installed. Displawall® can be installed over drywall. Visit Marlite's website for detailed installation instructions.

Accessories include 1" to 12" hooks and brackets, shelves, racks, Lucite holders, bins and baskets. Many of the products designed for retail stores are adaptable for garage storage.

Designed for the retail industry, Displawall® is not available at the local hardware store. Look in the yellow pages of the local telephone book for "Store Fixtures" or "Display- Fixtures & Material." These types of stores cater to retailers for their merchandising equipment needs.

All Marlite products are trademarks of Commercial & Architectural Products, Inc.

Solid colors to woodgrains, **DISPLAWALL**™ is coated with a laminate finish.

GarageGrids®

66 Highland Avenue
Newton, MA 02460
877.GARAGEGRIDS (427.2434)
Office 617.916.1255   www.GarageGrids.com

Here's a wall organizer that's versatile, durable, and easy to install. It's especially great for the garage. GarageGrids® is made with steel yet it weighs only 20 pounds per 2′ X 6′ panel. Install horizontally or vertically for whatever space in the home that requires storage.

The scratch-resistant steel is coated with white epoxy. Placement of the accessories is easy; so it's very versatile when storage needs change. Accessories include a variety of brackets, hooks, and baskets that can store most household items. The baskets have been tested to hold up to 60 pounds.

GARAGEGRIDS™ are easy to install on the garage wall, and it's great for other rooms of the house.

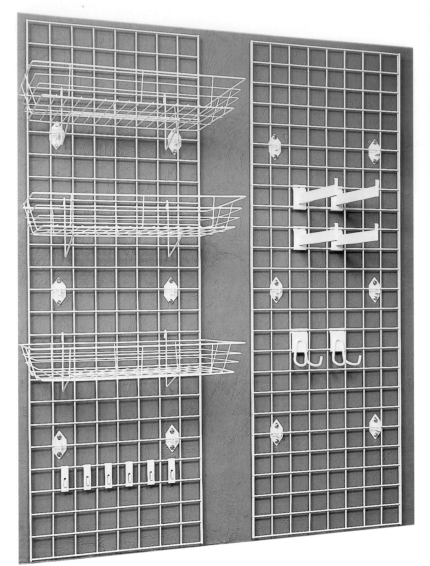

These heavy-duty hooks slip in and are secured on the grid panel like all **GARAGEGRIDS™** accessories.

You'll receive two, 2' x 6' panels plus the accessories you see here with each order. The panels can be mounted vertically or horizontally.

Most garage door companies distribute GarageGrids® products. This growing network of distributors will install the product too, or you can install the product yourself.

Each panel attaches to the studs with six wall mounts using twelve, 5/16" lag bolts.

Here's what you get when you place an order. Of course, additional accessories can be purchased.

- **2 Grid Panels (24" X 72")**
- **2 Heavy Duty Hooks**
- **4 Brackets 12"**
- **12 Wall Mounts**
- **3 Wire Baskets 24" W x 15" L x 4" D**
- **6 Universal Hooks**

More accessories can be ordered when the need arises. You can store anything weighing less than 80 pounds. GarageGrids® can be installed in other areas of the home such as the laundry room, children's rooms, basement storage, and garden shed.

THE FLOOR: EPOXY COATINGS & FLOOR COVERING

New and advanced floor products inspire the garage remodeler and organizer. Epoxy coatings are cheered and jeered; some application results are outstanding and other outcomes are miserable. Most epoxy coatings are pricey. Some manufacturers recommend that application be done by a professional painter. Understanding the product is crucial. Don't buy epoxy floor paint *only* based on price.

There are dozens of floor coatings available; there are more than I have time to research. Consult with local paint dealers for their ideas about epoxy coatings. Ask for references from people who have coated their garage floors with various products. Check with owners whose floors have been coated for at least a year. Go see them for yourself. Most home owners will be happy to show off their floors.

An innovative alternative to coating the floor is covering the floor. It is like driving the car onto the family rec room floor.

I expect more innovative flooring as garage remodeling and organizing becomes more popular.

Better Life Technology, LLC

9820 Pflumm Road, Lenexa, KS 66215

877.810.6444

Office 913.894.0403   www.bltllc.com

The rib channel parking pad is perfect to cover the entire garage floor.

Parking Pad™ Garage Floor Protector

Better Life Technology makes extraordinary garage floor covering products. What's extraordinary is the material used for its products. It is a specially-formulated polyvinyl that resists stains and contaminants commonly found in the garage.

It works. I placed a phosphoric-based acid wash, motor oil, antifreeze, and grease on a sample of the Parking Pad™ material for 10 days. Each item washed off leaving no tell-tale signs.

The Parking Pad™ in my garage is 7 1/2' X 17'. Even though my garage floor is coated with epoxy, I roll out my pad in the winter to protect the floor from four, studded snow tires. The pad shows no signs of punctures! It is easy to clean because of the channel design that allows water to flow or be swept away easily. Admittedly, there is one stain; the type of stain is unknown. But save for that one exception the Parking Pad™ cleans like new.

The other standard Parking Pad™ sizes are 9' X 20' and 10' X 22'. Custom lengths are also available in widths up to 10'. The standard width is 4' in the flooring industry for this type of product. Garage size varies, so a cut-to-fit Parking Pad™ is good news.

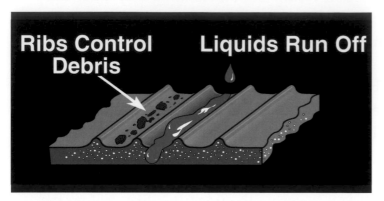

It's easy to cover the entire garage floor surface with the slip-resistant Parking Pad™ material, and there's no need to apply an adhesive on the floor. Each 10'-wide mat includes an additional 4" flap that can overlap each other. These flaps can be cut off with a utility knife, and the edges butt together to create a seam. Applying an adhesive or double-sided tape along the flap line is optional. But there is no requirement to use an adhesive if the product is placed over the entire garage floor surface. If you decide to use an adhesive, Better Life Technology reports that their customers claim Liquid Nails™ or OATY X 15 are effective adhesives.

This cleverly-designed pad is convenient to clean with a broom or wash with a garden hose. This specially-formulated polyvinyl is tough and durable yet supple to the touch.

G-Floor™ Garage Floor Protector

The heavy-duty big brother to the Parking Pad™ is the G-Floor™. This product is about double the thickness and comes in either the channel design or the attractive 'coin' design.

The G-Floor™ is cost-competitive when comparing it to an epoxy coating. Installation is also much faster than painting.

The G-Floor™ possesses the same qualities as the Parking Pad™. This durable material cushions any floor surface. And the coin-pattern design looks great when it's installed in other areas of the house such as a workshop, laundry room, basement storage room, rec room in the basement, bonus room above the garage, outside storage shed, and even a wine cellar. The possibilities are endless.

The Parking Pad™ and G-Floor™ are available in a variety of colors that include Slate Grey, Sandstone, Brick Red, Forest Green, Racing Blue, and Black. The product is available in a gloss or satin finish.

Contact the company for a distributor near you or for more information. The corporate office accepts orders when there are no distributors in your area.

Floor preparation tips before coating the garage floor with epoxy

Inadequate floor surface preparation is the result of 70% of all floor coating failures. A high-quality epoxy coating product could appear to have failed when, in fact, the surface is poorly prepared. So here are some important tips:

- **Wear safety goggles.**

- **Don't use muriatic acid for etching**. Even when thoroughly rinsed from the surface,
  muriatic acid residue is active and continues to eat away the concrete.

- **Use Rust-Oleum's Industrial Pure Strength 3599™ cleaner and degreaser.** This environmentally-friendly degreaser eliminates concentrations of oil and other automotive fluids. It is 100% concentrated. The product is non-caustic, non-abrasive, and non-acidic. Follow manufacturer's instructions.

- **Another Rust-Oleum product** that I have used is the 108 Cleaning and Etching™ Solution.

- **First, use a stiff bristle brush** or a heavy-duty steel brush to tackle the built up concentrations of grease and grime.

- **Use the etching solution to clean and prepare the rest of the garage floor.** Allow two days to dry completely after thoroughly rinsing with water before coating the floor with epoxy.

- **Do a final broom sweep** prior to the epoxy coating application.

- **Check with a local paint store** representative for additional information.

Here are a few commonly asked questions regarding epoxy application

Q: **We built a new home. Does the new concrete require acid etching?**
A: Yes. New concrete requires 30 days to cure to eliminate the alkaline. Acid etching creates a good bonding surface.

Q: **How long must I wait before I can drive my car onto the newly epoxy-coated garage floor?**
A: I recommend at least 14 days. That is more than most manufacturers recommend. But waiting a longer time allows for the new surface to cure completely.

Q: **My garage floor had an epoxy coating years ago. I would like to give it a fresh coat. Can I do that?**
A: Yes, but some preparation is required. Whether the epoxy is latex or oil-based, get a buffing machine with a heavy-duty sanding pad. Be sure to scarify the entire surface. Where tire tracks exist, completely remove the old epoxy from the concrete surface, acid etch, rinse and let dry for two days before applying a fresh coat.

While I have chosen not to review a myriad of floor coatings, the following two are excellent products based on personal experience.

TRU-GLAZE-WB™ 4408 by ICI Devoe

925 Euclid Avenue
Cleveland, OH 44115
(888) 424-2847   www.DevoeCoatings.com

TRU-GLAZE-WB™ 4408 is a two-part waterborne epoxy that is easy to apply and results in a high-gloss finish. I like the waterborne epoxies over the solvent-based ones because they are environmentally friendly and produce minimal odor. Use warm, soapy water for clean up.

The stain-resistant finish is easy to clean with a wet mop. But the surface tends to be slippery when wet. The company's specification sheet recommends adding one pound of pumice or other texturing material to each gallon of epoxy to aid traction. My experience shows that applying a specific texturing material over a fresh application of epoxy on the floor is a better solution. Clumps tend to form when added to the can of epoxy making the application somewhat irregular in spots.

After preparing the floor, use a clean, medium, synthetic nap roller with a long handle for application. Be sure to remove loose fibers in the nap of a new roller.

Following manufacturer's instructions, slowly mix Component B to Component A on a 1:1 ratio. Stir thoroughly and scrape the sides of the can to ensure proper mixing. Let the epoxy stand for 45 minutes at temperatures below 70°F before use. If the temperature is higher than 70°F, allow only 30 minutes induction time. This material is usable within six to eight hours, but always stir again prior to using. Never apply this epoxy when the surface or air temperature is less than 50°F.

ICI Devoe recommends applying two coats of this product. It is dry to the touch in two hours after application, but allow the floor to dry thoroughly overnight before adding a second coat and avoid any type of vehicular traffic at this time. In some cases, one coat may be sufficient depending on the application method and desired thickness. If two coats are used, the first coat should be a thinned application. This method ensures better bonding of the product to the floor.

After 48 hours, light foot traffic is permissible. But low temperature, high humidity, thickness of application, or poor ventilation will add to the time for curing. Yellowing can occur if there is a lack of ventilation or if portable fuel burning heaters are used during application and in the curing stages. The company's specifications suggest that full curing occurs in about seven days. Once again, I prefer 14 days for curing. The longer time compensates for weather variations that can affect the cure rate.

Now that you're primed to coat your floor with TRU-GLAZE-WB™ 4408, I must make a confession. The lab at ICI Devoe recommends that this product should not be used where there is vehicular traffic, which directly refers to the garage. Here's what I have discovered.

Gordon Shockley, from Aurora, Colorado coats garage floors for a living. His company, Concrete Painters, coats garage floors everyday and has for over five years. He's coated nearly 700 garage floors! Here's his secret. He applies one coat of TRU-GLAZE-WB™ 4408, and a coat of ICI Devoe's 126 Devran Clearcoat. The clear coat protects the color coat. He offers a five-year guarantee on his work.

Mr. Shockley also offers a three-coat option using one coat of TRU-GLAZE-WB™ 4408 and two coats of the 126 Devran Clearcoat. He offers a 10-year guarantee on the three-coat process.

"I've used just about everybody's product. Now I wouldn't use any other product," said Mr. Shockley commenting on the ICI Devoe's products.

Consult an ICI Devoe coatings specialist for further information before you coat your garage floor.

7100 Envira-Poxy™ by Kelly-Moore Paint Co., Inc.

987 Commercial Street
San Carlos, CA 94070
Office 800.874.4436 www.KellyMoore.com

Envira-Poxy™ is a water-based two-part epoxy that is environmentally friendly. It was made for the production facilities of Boeing Aircraft. It worked so well in an industrial setting that the product was introduced for general use in 1992. This product is time-tested.

This product works similarly to the ICI Devoe product. Mix Component 'A' with Catalyst 'B'. This product has a pot life (working time) of four to six hours.

Broadcast their texturing material called Shark Grip immediately following a fresh application of Envira-Poxy™ to create a slip-resistant surface.

Kelly-Moore recommends a two-coat process. It dries in two hours and it's ready for the second coat in six hours. Allow the second coat to dry for 16 hours for light foot traffic. After 72 hours, light vehicular traffic, such as bicycles, is permissible.

There's no strong odor with Envira-Poxy™. It cleans up with warm, soapy water. The result is a high-gloss shine, and it can be cleaned with a wet mop to maintain that shine over time.

Kelly Moore is located in 10 Western states.

Winter gunk finds its way into the garage, but…

…cleanup is quick and easy with **Kelly-Moore's Envira-Poxy™** coating the floor surface.

THE CEILING: THE FORGOTTEN SPACE

Seasonal items or other household objects used infrequently can efficiently be stored from the garage ceiling or rafters. Explore this forgotten space to get more objects off the floor and out of the way. For example, the ceiling may be the perfect spot for those items you cannot part with and never use. At least by storing those objects from the ceiling, clutter is reduced. Holiday decorations, off-season tires, patio accessories, and a host of other items can be stored out of the way but remain visible when needed.

Be cautious and avoid overloading ceiling storage especially in older garages. Most ceilings will support some storage. But trusses have limitations like all structural components in the home. Moderation is a key. If you're concerned about the structure, consult with a professional for peace of mind.

Hyloft USA, LLC

5175 West Diablo Drive
Suite 110, Las Vegas, NV 89118
Toll-free 866.249.5638
Office 702.254.6900   www.Hyloft.com

Hyloft® storage platforms are made specifically for the garage ceiling. This award-winning product has the versatility to be used anywhere in the house. This type of storage system allows bulky items to be stored that can't be stored in traditional cabinets or shelves.

Each storage unit is 45" X 45" and has a load capacity up to 250 pounds. The scratch-resistant steel platforms can be set as close as 16" from the ceiling. This is helpful where ceilings are low. The adjustable down rods that attach to the ceiling allow the platform to hang up to 28" from the ceiling. Just one unit creates storage potential of over 30 cubic feet.

The smaller version is the Hyloft Jr. Storage Unit. This 36" X 36" unit can be used in smaller areas such as laundries, pantries, and closets.

Each order includes installation instructions. To learn how easy it is to install Hyloft units, go to the company's website.

The company offers hanging accessories for tools, ladders, baskets, and hooks designed to attach to the bottom of the Hyloft units.

Hyloft products can be obtained through the company's website. Some Hyloft storage units can be found at Home Depot, Do-It-Best Centers, Wal-Mart Supercenters, Target, Sam's Club, Meyer, and Lowes.

The **Hyloft** works well in just about any room where you desire to leverage your storage options.

Hyloft is a smart storage solution: You're only steps away from what you've stored, but It's never In your way. Now that's a great Idea!

GarageTek® and Whirlpool® Corporation champion the crusade to reinvent the Great American Garage

Two prominent national companies lead the way in helping home owners to reinvent their garages. Start up GarageTek® and corporate giant Whirlpool® Corporation have developed their own proprietary product lines to completely furnish and accessorize residential garages. Each company in its own way is impacting this nascent industry.

GarageTek®

The idea for GarageTek® was hatched in 2000 when company founders Marc Shuman and Skip Barrett were traveling through the hinterlands of Texas after having met with a corporate client. At the time, both men were employed by International Visual Corporation, a manufacturer of store fixtures and visual merchandising equipment. IVC had recently developed what is known today as Tek Panel. Tek Panel was designed to replace the medium density fiberboard slatwall that many retailers use to display merchandise.

The quest was on to expand the uses for Tek Panel. Marc and Skip probed various industries looking for new applications for this innovative product. Numerous ideas were bantered between the two. Then Marc remembered a store that sold an assortment of products to organize residential garages. From this idea, came a flash of inspiration both men embraced. Tek Panel was the foundation on which other products could be developed to furnish an entire garage. After several months of intense market research, the business model was built. New York-based GarageTek® began selling complete garage-furnishing systems to the public in 2001.

Wouldn't you prefer a clean, functional, and organized garage?

GarageTek® distributes its products through its franchise system. Franchises sold quickly in the Eastern states. Now the company is rapidly selling franchises throughout the country. Stiff competition exists in some regions where franchisee-hopefuls vie for the opportunity to own a GarageTek® franchise.

A home owner can contact a local GarageTek® representative to obtain a custom layout and design at no charge. The layout and design include a wide selection of shelving, cabinets, and accessories that the home owner chooses to furnish the garage completely. Most installations can be completed in a day or two.

These tall cabinets can be moved to wherever **Tek Panel®** is installed.

The workbench can serve each member of the family for hobbies, crafts, projects, repairing equipment and so much more!

Store it high and away for seldom-used items to conserve valuable wall space.

Imagine being able to store conveniently virtually anything off the floor. This sampling of accessories from **GARAGETEK®** shows their versatility and how easy they are to use.

Whirlpool® Corporation - Gladiator™ GarageWorks

Whirlpool® Corporation launched a world-wide initiative in 1999 to create innovative products to differentiate it from competitors and to make customers' lives easier. Among the new products resulting from that global effort emerged Gladiator™ GarageWorks, a complete system of organizing products and a line of appliances made especially for the garage. The product design features steel, treadplate fronts.

Todd Starr, product development director for Whirlpool® Corporation, noted the "frustration home owners live with about their garage." He went on to say: "The garage is the area in the home that is ripe with opportunity to provide a comprehensive line (of products) that is an integrated and a modular system for storing food and beverage among other household items."

Some of those products include a modular workbench that's 8' feet wide with a 1 1/2" solid maple surface. The design allows for mobile modular units to slide beneath the workbench. The GearDrawers and GearBox are modular units for storage. Even one model of its Garage Refrigerator is known as the "beer box" can slip beneath the workbench.

GearWall™ is the wall organizing system made from extruded plastic panels with grooves that accommodate hanging a variety of household goods. There's even the Garage Compactor and the Freezerator™.

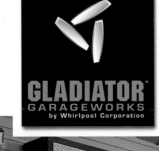

Gladiator™ GarageWorks General Manager Tom Arent said, "Families want to feel as good about their garage as they do about their house, yard, car or boat. They can start with just a modular workbench, transform the entire garage in one step, or settle for something in between."

The Gladiator™ GarageWorks products are distributed through Lowe's, Sears, and a network of distributors.

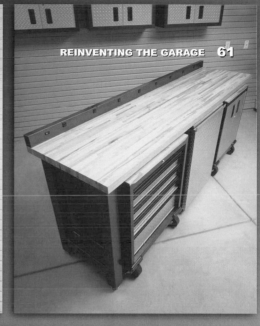

The Tall **GearBox** and locker are built on casters providing mobility which offers flexibility for your storage needs.

The **GearWall Panels** lets you store objects off the floor, and they are easy to see when you need them.

This rugged **Workbench** features a 1 1/2" maple work top.

Who knows appliances better than Whirlpool®? The **Freezerator** is specially designed for the garage along with other garage appliances.

The **GearRack** enables you to move supplies, parts, or tools to the project in the garage that you are working on.

Whirlpool's® refrigerator shown as the **BeerBox** means refreshment is always close at hand in the garage.

"That's what your house is,
a place to keep your stuff while you go out
and get…more stuff!
Sometimes you gotta move, gotta get a bigger house.
Why? No room for your stuff anymore."
—George Carlin, *Stuff*

A CASE STUDY IN REINVENTING THE GARAGE

For Doug and Sue Carter of Greeley, Colorado, the day had arrived to conquer the mountains of clutter in their garage. Doug is an eye surgeon and Sue is a gynecologist. Three of their four children reside at home, and all members of the family are heavily engaged in sports and outdoor activities. Their 1,000-square-foot garage was designed to accommodate three cars, but so far it had been used exclusively as an oversized sports locker and for much more as the photo above illustrates.

Doug and Sue had dreams of an organized system that would allow them to fit everything—even the cars—into the garage. As both busy doc-

As both busy doctors and full-time parents, they had neither the time nor the inclination to tackle this daunting task alone.

tors and full-time parents, they had neither the time nor the inclination to tackle this daunting task alone. Doug was aware of my book, *Your Garagenous Zone: The Complete Garage Organizer Guide*, and he made an appointment to determine how I might help them meet their objective. Professional organizer Kathy Lanning accompanied me on our initial appointment to evaluate the situation.

As we exchanged introductions, Doug explained that they were in the process of completing some other renovation projects and the garage was next in line for a complete makeover. Acknowledging the area's current state of disarray, Doug offered apologies—unnecessary of course, since the disorganization was the reason we were there, but nonetheless, very common from homeowners.

If the Colorado Tourism Board needs a poster family for outdoor activities, these folks would be a shoo-in.

Traversing the goose decoys, sports equipment, and other outdoor gear, we considered our options for breathing new life into the space. Doug explained the various activities in which each family member is engaged. He is captain of a local hockey team, while Sue is the cross-country coach at a local high school and the speed coach for a local track club, and also enjoys scuba diving. Their three children living at home are also active in athletics. Tori, 17, is a national incline speed-skating champion and a member of the state championship cross-country team; Cameron, 15, participates in wrestling, track, cross-country, and motocross; and Spencer, 13, plays basketball, ski blades, and is involved in robotics.

All family members participate in skiing (both snow and water), fly fishing, hunting, dog training, hockey, and snowboarding. If the Colorado Tourism Board needs a poster family for outdoor activities, these folks would be a shoo-in.

STOP! in the name of clutter!

Identify the needs

In formulating a comprehensive plan for any garage overhaul, the first step is learning about the activities of the people using the space. Once we had accomplished that step with the Carters, we were ready to begin identifying specific needs. Here is what we discovered:

Has anybody seen my skates?

- The majority of their activities are water-related, so the type of storage to be added must take this into account. Storage of wet gear can lead to mold and mildew. This problem can be avoided with selection of the proper cabinet material.

- Doug alerted us to the need for counter space to serve as a work bench and as an area for sorting and organizing equipment.

- With hunting among their activities, this family wanted a deep, stainless-steel sink in the garage for dressing small game, a task they would rather not perform in the kitchen sink.

- Maximizing as much storage space as possible was a clear focus for the Carter family. We noted that the ceiling height, at a generous 10.5 feet, would allow many vertical storage options.

- Creating space that is easy to maintain and to clean was also important to the Carters. They hoped to spend a lot of time in the garage, so they wanted it to be an inviting, enjoyable area.

- The garage walls would be ideal for a system to organize garden implements, brooms, ladders, and other tools typically found in a garage.

- The doorway leading from the house to the garage presented a special challenge. This area features a 30-inch-high landing and steps leading down to the garage floor, but it had no railing. We endeavored to use this space creatively and remedy the existing safety hazard at the same time.

The Mission Statement

Once the family's needs were pinpointed, the next step was to put together a mission statement to direct the planning of the garage overhaul. In this case, we determined that our mission was to modify the garage interior to maximize the efficient use of the space, to add categorized storage areas so the family's various sporting equipment could be found with ease, to put systems in place that would allow for safety and easy cleaning, and to reclaim space to park the family cars.

... our mission was to modify the garage interior to maximize the efficient use of the space, to add categorized storage areas so the family's various sporting equipment could be found with ease...

Design the Plan

Once the activities, needs, and mission were identified, we got to work.

Having completed these steps with Doug and Sue, we sketched a plan, making modifications until it met their expectations. As in any construction project, the importance of crystallizing the vision of the end result in the home owners' minds is paramount for ultimate satisfaction. A verbal-only overview of the impending work can lead to disastrous results. The home owner might be unable to picture the final outcome through discussion alone and could easily end up dissatisfied. Working with more than one person, as we were with the Carters, compounds that risk. Getting everything on paper is therefore a crucial step.

The backless cabinets offered more storage options with the **DISPLAWALL™** mounted on the wall.

To complete the final design for the Carters' garage, we worked with local carpenters Marty Tjelmeland and V. J. Elliott, and with Bob Yost, a distributor for two product lines of garage cabinets in Colorado. Both carpenters are experienced in garage makeovers and were familiar with the products used in this project, which helped the project to move forward smoothly.

Cabinets & Pantries

There is great variety in the garage cabinets on the market today, both in options and in price. Depending on which products are chosen, a project like the Carters' could cost upward of $20,000. Fortunately, more affordable options can be found without sacrificing quality.

The Carters chose cabinets manufactured by Mitchell Garage Cabinet Systems in Stillwater, Oklahoma (see Products and Costs at the end of this chapter). This company's wide selection of sizes enabled the Carters to implement a modular approach and to choose cabinets that would fit well into their newly reclaimed space. Made of furniture-grade particle board with medium-density fiberboard doors, these cabinets arrive unpainted to allow buyers to finish them according to their preferences. Thinking of the wet equipment they planned to store, the Carters chose to paint their cabinets to make them resistant to moisture. We also recommended that they label each section of closed storage once they had decided what would go where.

The cabinet boxes are constructed with rugged dovetail joints and are backless, with the wall serving as the back surface of each cabinet. Installation is easy and secure: Each cabinet hangs on a steel rail affixed horizontally to the wall and can support a load of up to 300 lbs.

Using cabinets that hang above the floor rather than resting on it offers several important advantages in a garage. All garage floors slant to the garage opening to promote water drainage, and they also tend to shift over time due to movement of the underlying soil and the weight of automobiles. Since the floor is by nature uneven, shelves or cabinets resting on it cannot be leveled easily or attractively. Hanging the cabinets above the floor solves this problem, and it also allows the homeowner to sweep or hose off the entire garage floor when cleaning.

Custom Workbench

The workbench becomes a central feature of any well-appointed garage because it serves multiple purposes for every member of the family. The length of this space in the Carters' garage is 10'; four feet of which was consumed by the new sink.

The recommended height for this workbench is 40 inches, which is a special design characteristic. Most workbenches tend to be 30 or 36 inches tall. For many

Organize to visualize.

people, this leads to stooping slightly while working on a project, which strains the lower back. When designing a workbench, therefore, take into consideration the height and comfort of the people who will be using it. A taller workbench also provides a higher storage area beneath, allowing more room for tall items such as a wet/dry vac or trash receptacle.

Wall Organizer System

A basic premise in organization is to create a visual stimulus. In other words, organize to visualize: If you can see it, you can find it. For the Carters, Displawall by Marlite was the way to accomplish this goal.

Displawall is a product used in retail stores. Each 4' x 8' sheet is a grooved panel made from medium-density fiberboard which is attached to the wall by screwing it into the studs. Removable hooks of varying lengths are then added, allowing for flexible, changeable storage. We used nine Displawall sheets in this project, creating 288-square-feet of storage space. Displawall features a durable, laminate finish that cleans easily, and it comes in a variety of colors. The Carters chose the almond colored finish to coordinate with their space and to create a light, bright environment.

Displawall panels and accessories can be found at stores that cater to retail store owners. A list of distributors is provided on the company's website (see Products and Costs).

Floor Coating

The Carters wanted a garage floor surface that would clean up easily. Garage floors are exposed to an onslaught of dripping and staining automotive fluids along with the typical grime that is either rolled into the garage by car tires or brought in by foot. Much of this debris finds its way into the home.

The Carters wanted a garage floor surface that would clean up easily.

Many floor paints or epoxies simply do not withstand the test of time and begin to chip, flake, or blister after about six months. In my experience, however, Envira-Poxy by Kelly-Moore Paints is up to the task. Envira-Poxy is a two-part, water reducible, environmentally friendly coating. The manufacturer recommends professional application of this product. While battleship gray seems to be the color of choice among many homeowners who paint their garage floors, the Carters agreed with our suggestion to use a lighter color for a more visually pleasing result.

Envira-Poxy creates a durable finish and a surface that cleans easily with a wet mop. The surface can become slippery when wet, but a product called H & C Shark Grip can be integrated into the application of Envira-Poxy to reduce slippage.

Kelly-Moore Paint stores are located west of the Mississippi River. A comparable product, Tru-Glaze-WB 4408 by Devoe Paints, is available nationally. (See Products and Costs for both.)

This landing extends 30" above the garage floor posing a safety hazard. An innovative idea solves the safety hazard by installing storage cabinets and a handrail. This pleased Sue and everyone in the family.

PHOTOGRAPHY BY A.B. FOORMAN ©2003

Adding Safety and More Storage

The final task in the Carters' project was to remedy a safety hazard that existed when entering the garage from inside the house. The 30-inch landing with four steps down to the garage floor required a handrail to conform with local building codes. This space also provided an opportunity to build in additional pantry space for staple goods. To eliminate the safety hazard, we installed a pantry cabinet next to the stairs and attached a handrail to the cabinet.

The Carters' "New" Garage

The Carter family can now enjoy their dream garage: They're able to find everything and fit everything in. Sue was impressed with the accessibility of the stored items. "Now all we have to do is grab it and go," she remarked. Doug was pleased with the recovery of the space's original function: "Before we couldn't get any of our cars in the garage," he noted. Sue was also vastly relieved that small game will no longer be processed in the house. "Having the sink in the garage will eliminate a huge, smelly mess in the kitchen," she commented. Doug summarized their overall satisfaction: "It is so nice to come home and not see a disaster."

"It is so nice to come home and not see a disaster."

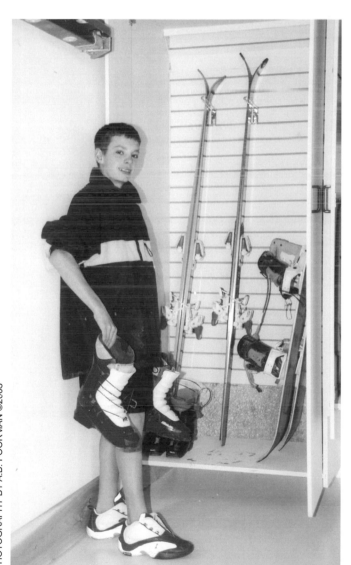

Spencer can find his sporting equipment with ease.

PHOTOGRAPHY BY A.B. FOORMAN ©2003

PHOTOGRAPHY BY A.B. FOORMAN ©2003

The Carter family beaming with delight over their "new" garage.

Function and organization create an intended outcome or purpose. That purpose provides usable space, efficient storage with eye-popping appeal, which are meaningful results for the garage environment.

Mitchell Garage Cabinet Systems

800.350.6427

www.mitchellgaragecabinetsystems.com

Cost of the Carters' Selections:

Cabinets: $2,200   Installation: $1,900

Paint and Labor: $800

TOTAL: $4,900

Custom Workbench

Cost of the Carters' Selections:

Workbench: $200   Stainless steel sink: $400

Plumbing: $500

TOTAL: $1,100

Displawall by Marlite

330.343.6621

www.displawall.com

Cost of the Carters' Selections:

Materials: $600   Labor: $350

TOTAL: $950

Envira-Poxy by Kelly-Moore Paints

www.kellymoore.com

OR

Tru-Glaze-WB 4408 by Devoe Paints

www.devoepaint.com

H & C Shark Grip

Available online from Aubuchon Hardware

www.aubuchonhardware.com

Cost of the Carters' Selections:

EPOXY: $800   Labor: $500

TOTAL: $1,300

Custom Handrail and Additional Pantry for the Landing Area

Cost of the Carters' Selections:

Framing & Cabinets: $320   Labor: $115

TOTAL: $435

*The total cost for this project
was $8,685, just under $9 per square foot.
Note that the cost of similar projects will
vary by region.*

Panel Styles & Fenestrations

Illustrations by
Robert Leanna

Sliding (1910-1929)

Swinging (1910-1940)

With Wicket Door (1915-1929)

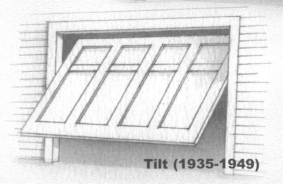

Sectional Overhead (1921-present)

Folding (1915-1929)

Tilt (1935-1949)

THE GARAGE DOOR & OPENERS:
The largest entry into the house

Selecting a garage door

The evolution of garage doors reflects major changes in the last hundred years. Acceleration of change is occurring more rapidly in recent years. Driven to maintain and expand market share and consumer demand, garage door manufacturers innovate to compete.

Many options are available if you are building a new home and looking for a garage door, or if you are considering replacing a garage door.

During a recent International Builders' Show, 11 of 12 garage door manufacturers revealed prototypes for carriage house-style doors. Companies exist that make only designer garage doors to satisfy the custom home market. The appetite among home owners is growing for eye-appealing garage doors, but consider too the construction features for a quality-made door.

- Steel doors are strong and secure. Quality doors are made with 24-gauge steel that is dent resistant. The lower the number, the thicker the steel. Some garage-door makers tout that their doors are made with "nominal 25-gauge" steel, which actually means thinner steel. The difference is relatively small, but look for "true 24-gauge" steel doors.

- Hot-dip galvanization is preferred over electro-galvanization. The hot-dip method completely coats the steel doors to prevent rust.

- An insulated, double steel skin door means the outside and inside are steel and the middle is a polystyrene or polyurethane core. The exterior and interior steel panels are bonded with the core insulation for durability. Most doors are two inches thick and provide excellent insulation.

- Look for sectional panels that are constructed with a pinch-resistant design. The U. S. Consumer Product Safety Commission reports that nearly 9,000 finger injuries are associated with garage doors every year.

- Choose torsion springs over extension springs. Torsion springs divide the weight of the door evenly making it easier to raise. Torsion springs contribute to a door's longevity and are far safer than extension springs.

- Nylon rollers that run along the track are quieter than steel rollers.

- Better-made doors include full-width vinyl bubble weather stripping on the base of the door to seal out weather.

I recommend hiring professionals for installing garage doors. But be sure to hire a reputable company. Ask for company referrals from friends and neighbors who have had good results. Scams do occur even to the extent that fraudulent "companies" will buy yellow page ads promising to install doors and openers they are not authorized to sell. Be cautious about those deals that are too good to be true.

Selecting a garage door opener

Imagine arriving home in your driveway, stopping the car, getting out to unlock the garage door, opening the door, returning to the car, driving into the garage, and finally closing the garage door. Fortunately, this five-step process is a thing of the past. Small conveniences like the garage door opener loom large when absent from the daily routine. When the opener is beyond repair and it's time to buy a new one, here are some helpful suggestions to avoid "down time."

Small conveniences like the garage door opener loom large when absent from the daily routine.

Many brands of garage door openers exist on the market. But two manufacturers make the majority of openers. Chamberlain makes Craftsman, LiftMaster, and its own brand. Overhead Door makes the Genie brand. So when comparing features and prices, consider the manufacturer behind the brand to obtain a clear understanding how much that model costs.

All garage door openers since 1992 are required to include an automatic reversing mechanism to stop the door's closing movement when an object obstructs its path. The mechanism is controlled by an infrared beam near the floor. Today's door openers respond more quickly to an obstruction than openers from 10 years ago. If your garage door opener was installed before 1992, you should consider investing in a new and safer opener.

Three types of garage door openers are available:

1. *Chain-drive mechanism* is the most affordable and widely used.
2. *Screw-drive mechanism* operates with a long-threaded bar, which causes a door to open slowly.
3. *Belt-drive mechanism* is the most expensive and considered the quietest device.

New garage door openers include an innovative security feature. Each time the door opener operates, a new security code rolls into place. The transmitter and receiver possess a set unique combination of 1,000,000 random codes. That security is a tough code to crack for any would-be intruder.

> *Today's door openers respond more quickly to an obstruction than openers from 10 years ago.*

Another security and convenience feature is the multifunctional remote control unit. Several buttons on the remote unit control the door, a garage light, and even lights or appliances inside the house.

Also available are wireless keypads that attach to the outer frame of the garage door opening. This keyless entry is especially handy when you leave the house for a walk or bike ride and don't want to be bothered with carrying keys. These units are inexpensive.

Wayne-Dalton innovates with new garage door opener design

Garage door manufacturer Wayne-Dalton has developed the latest garage innovation with the *i*drive' garage door opener. The "*i*" in *i*drive™ must certainly stand for innovation.

This revolutionary garage door opener attaches to the wall above the door. It works in concert with the TorqueMaster™, Wayne-Dalton's unique spring system that's encloses the

springs inside a steel tube. When activated the opener turns the torsion tube to operate the door in a smoother fashion compared to traditional door openers.

This close up shows the springs in the steel tube in the **TorqueMaster™**.

Many homes utilize the traditional torsion springs. The *idrive*™ now works with most torsion-spring doors. Imagine, no clanking chains when operating the garage door opener. The *idrive*™ is quiet, safe, and convenient.

No special wiring is required among the wall button, overhead light, and the opener. The light plugs into a standard outlet within line-of-sight of the opener. No pre-wiring saves dollars. And if a power failure occurs, there's an emergency battery-powered back-up system.

Wayne-Dalton received first place for the 2003 Innovation Awards for their new opener from the *Home Improvement Executive,* a magazine directed to executive-level readers in the home improvement industry.

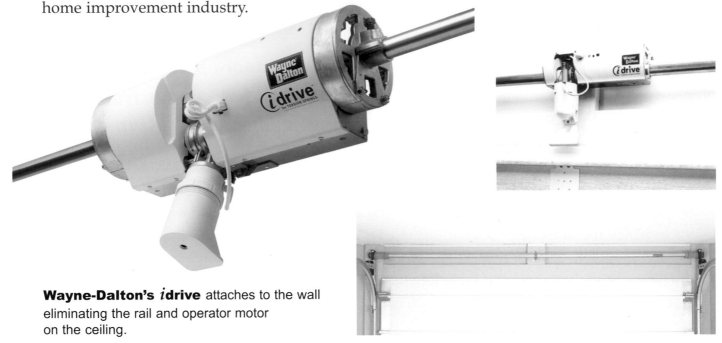

Wayne-Dalton's *i*drive attaches to the wall eliminating the rail and operator motor on the ceiling.

FrenchPorte LLC

121 Congressional Lane, Penthouse Suite, Rockville, MD 20852
Office 301.545.0400   www.FrenchPorte.com

FrenchPorte™ Garage Doors

"Absolute shock" were the words that Jennifer Maher used to describe the unattractive appearance of most garage doors that stimulated her desire to change the face on America's home front. Enhancing appearances is a talent for this veteran makeup artist for ABC News in Washington D.C. That's when she devised the clever and unique design of giving the look of French doors to her patented garage door design.

FrenchPorte™ Garage Doors is a sectional-type, overhead door made with heavy-walled aluminum alloy extrusion. The baked-on enamel produces a durable yet smooth finish. Stock colors are being formulated, but the door surface is paintable, so an exact match for any home's trim or body color is easy to attain. Painting the door requires painting in the future along with the rest of the home, which is routine maintenance for any home.

The window panes are made with a translucent polycarbonate material that is approximately 1/4" thickness. Natural lighting creates an inviting environment inside the garage, but visibility into the garage is extremely limited from the outside. Other advantages of using polycarbonate are the impact protection compared to glass or acrylic that tends to become brittle over time and the UV resistance creates an attractive application over other materials.

Optional door handles add to the finished look creating the appearance of authentic French doors. Door handles are available in either a brass or nickel finish.

I asked professional organizer Janet Hall to conduct a field study to file a first-hand report to help with research about the FrenchPorte™ Garage Doors. She summarized her report by saying, "The FrenchPorte™ Garage Doors really do make an impact and a difference. I fell in love with the look and would recommend the purchase and installation to any home owner looking to improve the appearance of their home." Janet's observations reflect the importance of appearance that author Virginia Postrel writes about in her book, *The Substance of Style*, when she says, "The boom in product design is just one sign of the increasing importance of sensory content in every aspect of life. Making people, places, and things look good is a growth business."

Other garage door companies are making changes to improve the appearance and design of their doors while other companies specialize in manufacturing only custom garage doors. But FrenchPorte™ Garage Doors is a significant entry into the field of innovative ideas for the garage.

Distributor opportunities are available from the company.

FrenchPorte™ doesn't eliminate the garage door; it only looks that way.

QUICK TIPS & PRODUCT IDEAS FOR THE WELL-APPOINTED GARAGE

During media interviews and when guests visit us, I often get the question, "Do you really park your cars in *this* garage?" My response is always, "Yes, of course, that's what the garage is for." Finally, I settled the issue by attaching a placard on the wall that reads, **"Yes, as a matter of fact, we *do* park our cars in the garage."**

But we use the garage for other activities too. We hosted our son's 7th birthday party in the garage. It's been the overflow room for a New Year's Eve party. Our garage was the site for a wine-tasting dinner that hosted 35 participants as a fund-raising event for our son's school. It was a big hit. We had a cigar night in the garage. It wasn't just any cigar night: It was a *Cigarage Night*. That's flex space.

Kid's birthday parties are great to host in the garage.

This wine tasting dinner for 35 served as a school fund raiser in the garage.

Besides this sampling of activities, here are some *quick* tips that are useful in the garage. File these ideas away. You may not need them right away, but some day they'll be helpful.

Casters

If you have a freezer or fridge in your garage, have you looked behind and under them lately? Chances are good that insects and spiders maintain extensive homes there! Appliances are too heavy to move to keep this area clean. Most appliance models include pre-drilled holes to screw in casters. Installing casters make cleaning easy, and you'll avoid inviting the nests of bugs and spiders.

Select the caster size that accommodates the weight of your appliance. Casters are available at hardware stores and home improvement centers.

Fitness center

Workout equipment can be bulky and consume a room in the house. Put the treadmill or stationery bicycle in your newly remodeled and organized garage. Do you get too warm working out? Open the garage door for fresh air. During winter in an insulated, unheated garage, temperatures seldom drop below freezing. Cooler temperature in the garage makes exercising comfortable. Most people get too hot exercising in the house—to say nothing of odiferous perspiration.

Today's treadmills can be folded and stored against a wall to save floor space. You might save a few dollars and a lot of time by having your personal gym at home too.

Wall-mounted television

Exercising can be boring. A wall-mounted television might add some entertainment to make the time fly by as you exercise. How about that nagging home improvement project you need to get done? With a TV in the garage, you can work and watch the Big Game.

Installing a wall-mounted swivel at a good vantage point for television viewing in the garage is easy. Wall-mounted swivels are available at discount stores and all home improvement centers.

Convert a part of your garage into a personal gym.

Message center

Install a dry board or chalk board strategically on the garage wall. When family members drive into the garage, they can see important messages. The message center is great for kids' artwork, for making a rough sketch of a home improvement project, making a list of needed supplies, brainstorming ideas, etc.

Telephone

Telephones are located in areas of the home for convenience. The garage is among the largest rooms in the home. So for convenience, install a phone in the garage. I especially enjoy having a cordless phone, so that I have the phone close by whether I am in the garage or venture into the yard.

Ceiling fan

If you enjoy being in the garage during the summer but can't bring yourself to install air conditioning, a ceiling fan can be a good alternative to beat the heat. Most fans move the air enough to keep the temperature comfortable.

Track lighting

Good lighting is critical for a multipurpose garage. It can be achieved by installing track lighting to replace the bare light bulb on a ceramic base. You will be de'lighted' with the results. A three-light track can make a huge difference and they cost only $25 in most home improvement centers.

Retractable extension cord

Messing around with extension cords is bothersome. That's why the retractable extension cord is appealing. Once the job is done, simply retract the cord into the housing unit. Most retractable cord products have lengths up to 30'. Determine the midway point in the garage where the extension will reach, and install it on the closest wall.

Storing a ladder

Many of today's homes are built with high ceilings. So the need exists for a tall step ladder. I installed two, Iron Wedge (model #PIW-1) bike hooks made by Racor in my garage. The ladder rests safely against the wall and off the floor. It's made for a bike, but it works for storing a ladder too.

Patching floor expansion joints

If you're considering coating or covering the garage floor, fill the expansion joints for a smooth finish throughout the garage. Typical concrete patch material will do. Let dry and gently sand the surface until it's flush with the garage floor.

By smoothing the entire floor, it is quick and easy to clean.

Another product option that works well to fill the joint is Bondo®. This product is made to fix car dents, but it also works in the expansion joints. It is harder to work with and to sand than concrete patch, but it provides a harder surface.

Don't be fooled. **RACOR** bike racks are great for hanging ladders too.

Protect your car door from support posts

Support posts in the garage are structural necessities. Their position can be in the path of opening the car door, which results in those barely noticeable, yet annoying dents. Steve Joblin, from Everything Garage, solves this nuisance in a very clever manner: He uses 4" plastic corrugated drain tubing. Using a utility knife, he cuts a slit along the pre-colored line from end to end. Because the tubing is flexible it fits easily around the support post. He created the instant bump guard. The flared end of the tubing is set on the floor.

He could use a carpet remnant or foam wrap, but for a clean look, the corrugated drain tubing is innovative. If black tubing is not your preferred color, clean the tubing, spray primer on the surface of the tubing and allow it to dry. Spray the tube with the color of your choice. Be sure to wear a mask when painting in a ventilated garage.

If you live in Pennsylvania, New Jersey, or Delaware, and you're interested in remodeling your garage contact Mr. Joblin at (215) 353-8699.

His website is www.EverythingGarage.com.

Wireless sound system

Wireless technology makes installing a sound system in the garage a simple job. Experiment with positioning the speakers for the best sound quality. If you own a wireless system for the home, add more speakers for the garage and fill the garage with tunes.

Stackable pet food storage

Pet stores and discount stores carry pet food storage containers that are stackable. Using one of the recommended wall organizing systems recommended in this book, you can stack storage containers on shelves or baskets and get pet food off the floor. If you have an open bag of pet food, it provides an open invitation for rodents and insects to go for the food.

Display your art!

It's likely you have some framed artwork stored in a closet or in a corner in the basement. Revisit that art, and hang some of it in the garage.

Stackable pet food containers off the floor help keep rodents away.

Enclose the stairway

In homes that have an open stairway from the garage leading into the house, dirt and debris collect under the stairs where it's tough to clean. Enclose the stairs and forget about sweeping there again.

Batteries & light bulbs

Batteries and light bulbs tend to be scattered in various locations throughout the house. When it's time to replace one of those items, locating the correct size or type can sometimes be elusive. Keep those items together in one location in a convenient spot in the garage.

The enclosed stairway is a clean look, and it keeps critters from nesting.

Racor® Home Storage Products

4100 McGee Road, Sandpoint, ID 83864
800.783.7725   www.RacorInc.com

Racor® Home Storage Products makes a variety of storage products. Visit the website for the complete line of products.

ProStor PBH-1 Hoist Monster

This bike hoist is made from solid steel construction. No assembly is required. When the non-abrasive hooks attach to the bicycle seat and handle bars, the hoist deploys a unique, rope locking mechanism that prevents accidental release.

ProStor PSB-2 Hangman Folding Bike Rack

Another bike storage option is the folding bike rack that attaches to the wall. It can serve also as a handy shelf even when the bikes are stored. Made with steel construction and epoxy finish, this product requires no assembly. Our family has used the folding bike rack for years.

All Racor® Home Storage Products are available in Ace Hardware, Tru-Serv, Pep Boys, and Bed Bath & Beyond.

The **Bike Slingger™** has a key lock for parental security.

Innovation has gone to great heights with the **Bike Slingger™**

Dale Campbell, Inventor

616 North Sheridan, Loveland, CO 80537

970.218.3050   Dale-c@msn.com

Bike Slingger™

Bike storage just got simpler. Mr. Campbell built a motorized hoist to make it easier for his wife to store her bike. This invention blossomed into a very useful garage product.

The motorized bike hoist is a clever idea to safely store bikes off the garage floor. The Bike Slingger™ uses easy-clip slings placed around the bicycle seat and handle bars. The key lock adds parental security. The easy-to-operate switch smoothly sends the hoist up or down. The load capacity is up to 70 pounds for all of the Slingger™ products.

The Bike Slingger Plus™ stores two bikes. But if you have surf boards, kayaks, canoes, or motorized scooters, this product can be used to accommodate storage of those too.

Everyone has stuff. The Stuff Slingger™ holds just about anything that typically occupies floor space or that's bulky or oddly shaped. The nylon-mesh net basket stretches, and it's secured to a 1/2" tubular, galvanized steel frame.

K & K, Inc.

28440 Glenview Drive, Elkhart, IN 46514,

Toll-free 866.869.5413

Office 574.266.8040   www.TheBikeBooster.com

Bike Booster

Nearly every member of today's active families is a bicycle enthusiast. Bicycles litter the garage floor. And it's even worse when a bike falls and scratches the paint on a parked car. The remedy is the Bike Booster.

The Bike Booster can elevate two bicycles off the floor safely regardless of ceiling height. The one-horse, hoist motor and heavy-duty nylon rope system provide a stable and quiet operation. The 110-V motor incorporates an automatic 'stop' mechanism to assure the bikes stop at the desired location near the ceiling.

Installation requires attic access to secure the Bike Booster on the ceiling of the garage for the desired location to store and retrieve bikes. Both bikes rise together during operation, but each bike is connected to an independent pulley system. This design assures a smooth operation and prevents bikes from becoming tangled or lodged together. I have seen the system work flawlessly. I could not detect any bike movement during operation.

The system works from a switch that is flush-mounted to the wall. The switch works only when it's activated. For safety, it is recommended to install the switch location high enough to be away from small hands. And, of course, avoid locating the switch near or beneath the Bike Booster. From a safety standpoint, the area should be clear while the Bike Booster operates.

Each bike is securely attached to a rubber-coated, stainless steel hook at the handle bars and the

The motorized **Bike Booster** lifts and stores bikes out of your way, yet they're easy to retrieve with the push of a button.

nylon rope loops around the saddle. To adjust the hooks and loop, simply loosen the rope release latch to accommodate the size of each bike. Then tug the rope to tighten the latch in place.

The entire unit is housed in a plastic outer body providing a seamless appearance. The Bike Booster is functional and unobtrusive. The weight capacity is 100 pounds, so you can store some canoes, kayaks, ladders, and a variety of objects that typically consume floor space. Contact the company for additional information.

The hook and loop devices secure the bike with a latch mechanism.

Bert Viskovich, Inventor

9035 Los Lagos Circle, Granite Bay, CA 95746
916.660.1656 www.ParkPerfect.com

This reflective optical device helps guide you to park in the same place in your garage every time.

Park Perfect Garage Parking Guide

The Park Perfect Garage Parking Guide product is one of those innovative ideas that makes you say, "I wish I had thought of that."

This specially-designed optical device allows you to park the car in the garage in the precise desired location every time. Park Perfect works for any vehicle and can be installed easily in minutes.

Here's how it works: Park the car in the desired location in the garage. Mount the Park Perfect in the vertical position on the back wall next to the garage door. Locate Park Perfect at the same height as the bottom edge of the tail light. Adjust the mirror so that you can see the brake light in the side-view mirror. That's it. When you park, look in your side-view mirror and stop when the tail light or brake light appears. You're home.

At present, the Park Perfect Garage Parking Guide can only be purchased from the website. I have them installed in our garage. As the name suggests, the car is parked perfectly in the same spot each time we arrive home. Distributorships are available from the inventor.

Pedestal Corporation

1114 East 6th Street, Emporia, KS 66801-3302

Office 620.343.2366 www.PedestalCorp.com

The Car Stop let's you park the car with laser beam accuracy every time.

Car Stop

Why not arrive home to a guided laser light show in the garage? The Car Stop points a laser beam on a predetermined spot on the car to let you know it's time to put on the brakes.

The laser emitter is mounted on the garage ceiling. Park the car in the desired location. Then adjust the laser beam to mark the exact spot where you want to stop. The sensor is mounted on the light cover of the garage door opener. When the door opener is operating, the light activates and triggers the laser light. My wife depends on her Car Stop each time she arrives home.

The Car Stop is carried in Sears stores, Home Depot, and a variety of catalogs and garage-related websites.

Chamberlain® Group, Inc.

Customer Service USA 800.528.2817

Canada 800.654.4736 www.Liftmaster.com

The garage door monitor lets you know inside your house when a garage door is left open.

Garage Door Monitor

It's 11:30 at night. I'm writing a magazine article in my study that overlooks the cul-de-sac. I spot my neighbor's garage door is open. My neighbors were awakened when I called—but they were appreciative. That event prompted me to check out the market for products that assure home owners their garage doors are closed. An open garage door is an open invitation for theft.

Liftmaster's® Wireless Garage Door Monitor is a small device that will provide you peace of mind. I keep my monitor on the bedside table. A little green light assures me that we won't be getting any calls from a neighbor telling me that our garage doors are open.

There are no special tools involved for installation. The sensor mounts on the garage door. The receiver can be located anywhere inside the house. When the garage door is open, the monitor light shines red. The receiver plugs into a standard 120V outlet. Up to four garage doors can be monitored with one receiver.

Liftmaster® products are available from garage door companies that carry Chamberlain® products.

The Lehigh Group

**2834 Schoeneck Rd.,
Macungie, PA 18062
610.966.9702   www.LehighGroup.com**

The **STOREHORSE SAWHORSE** will be your constant work companion for small to large projects. Two can hold up to 2000 lbs.

Storehorse Sawhorse

The old, clunky wooden sawhorse serves a purpose. But when you want to conserve space without compromising strength, the Storehorse is steady and sturdy.

This portable, plastic sawhorse is light-weight enough to carry anywhere. One pair can hold a hefty 2,000 pounds. The light-weight  Storehorse folds into 2" of space, which allows it to be stored on the wall of your garage. The Storehorse is light weight, but it's the heavyweight of sawhorses.

One model includes a special electric feature. The Cord 'n Plug includes a six-outlet center with 10' extension cord and reset switch. The feature is UL rated.

The Storehorse is carried in most hardware and building centers.

Narita Trading Company, Inc.,

154 Morgan Avenue, Brooklyn, NY 11237

800.775.2278 www.Shop-for-Housewares.com

Roll-out up to 175 pounds with **MY-CART**.

And when collapsed **MY-CART** hangs on the garage wall.

My-Cart

This luggage and utility cart totes up to 175 pounds. This product tackles smaller jobs than the Handee Truck 4 X 4, but its lightweight aluminum construction is just as durable for home and travel. Fully extended, My-Cart is 40" tall. When not in use, it is a compact 29" in height and only 2" thick—so it's easy to store on the wall. The sponge-grip handle makes handling easy. The toe plate and wheels open and close simultaneously.

I like to use My-Cart to tote landscaping material to a project or handle those 40-pound bags of dog food.

Visit the distributor's website to obtain either of these products. Or they are available at most Ace, Tru-Value, or Do-It-Best hardware stores, and through catalogs such as Improvements, and Hard to Find Tools.

Handee Truck 4 X 4

There's no need to fret about back strain when it's time to move a heavy object. The Handee Truck 4 X 4 is a versatile hand truck and dolly that weighs just 23 pounds. The aluminum construction holds a 250-pound load. The solid rubber tires and casters add to the sturdy dependability. The base is expandable from 20" to 35 1/2". Because it is collapsible, it can be easily stored on a wall and save valuable garage floor space.

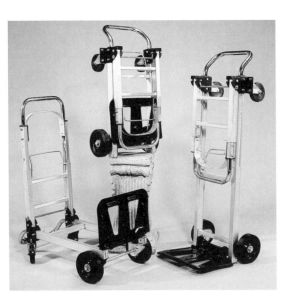

This versatile hand truck holds up to 250 pounds.

ODL Incorporated

215 East Roosevelt Avenue, Zeeland, MI 49464

Toll-free 800.253.3900   www.odl.com

No dangling blinds to clean because they're between two panes of glass. **Entry Point® Blinds** add a measure of security when installed on garage service doors.

Entry Point® Blinds

Security is paramount for the safety of your home and family. Any service door in the garage that exits into the backyard is an easy target for intruders, especially when there's a window. The window allows easy viewing into the garage to determine if anyone is home. When the cars are gone, burglars know that no one is home.

The steel or fiberglass entrance doors with windows and plastic frames can be secured with ODL's Entry Point® blinds. This window insert is double-paned with aluminum blinds installed between the panes of glass.

The blinds tilt open-and-closed with a horizontal, slide mechanism. The blinds can be raised and lowered with a vertical, squeeze-controlled button that moves up and down.

The window sizes that accommodate ODL's products are 20" X 36" and 22" X 36". The inserts are easy to install and they provide maximum privacy.

ODL makes a similar insert product for full-length windows. The sizes are 20" X 64" and 22" X 64".

With the blinds between the glass panes, washing the window is easy and no dangling or clanking blinds to be bothered with.

Solar Flair tubular skylight

ODL makes another product to bring natural light into a dark garage — the Solar Flair tubular skylight. These skylights also work well in other darkened rooms or hallways in the home. There are times you need to fetch an item from the garage. You won't need to turn on a light or open the garage door with a tubular skylight in place.

The 95% Reflective Film captures the light in the tube and disseminates it throughout the garage. A 10" tubular skylight covers about 150 square feet. A 14" skylight covers 300 square feet. That's a lot of coverage from a small opening.

Installation is made simple with the one-piece polyurethane flashing for asphalt roof applications. Other flashing material is available for high-profile and low-profile tile roofs.

Water Coil Hose, Inc.

26051 Merit Circle, Suite 106

Laguna Hills, CA 92653

949.367.9220   www.WaterCoilHose.com

The recoil memory of each
WATER COIL HOSE® will make you
wonder why you didn't own one sooner.
Available in a rainbow of colors.

Water Coil Hose®

A hose connected to a water supply in the garage is handy. Most hoses are bulky, hard to store, and easy to trip over. The Water Coil Hose® solves all these problems, and it's a great convenience anywhere around the house that you need a hose.

The Water Coil Hose® is made of 100% polyurethane, which creates a flexible hose with a "recoil" memory that simplifies storage. The hose is glossy and smooth to the touch. Similar hoses that 'pretend' to look like a Water Coil Hose® are made from low-quality materials that have a dull finish and feel rough.

The company produces a 25' or 50' hose with a 3/8" inside diameter. Another product is a 50' hose with a 1/2" inside diameter. The 1/2" hose delivers greater water pressure than the 3/8" model. Each hose is rated at 100 pounds per square inch.

The 50' hose is easy to use for washing the garage floor. And it stretches with ease to wash the car in the driveway.

The Water Coil Hose® is available in many hardware and discount stores and various catalogs.

Tivan, Inc.

5305 Frost Point
Prior Lake, MN 55372-1906
Office 952.440.8233   www.Loft-It.com

Loft-It™ Storage Lift System

Key switch provides for authorized users to operate the **Loft-It™**.

When it's on the floor…it's time to Loft-It™. This innovative invention lifts motorcycles, snow mobiles, riding lawnmowers, bicycles, ATVs, golf carts, and anything else up to 1,000 pounds that uses valuable floor space. If that weight limit is exceeded, the system does not operate.

Constructed with aircraft aluminum, the Loft-It™ platform is 4' X 8'. The platform can be elevated up to 6'. The motor-driven platform is key-operated. When the key is removed, there is no fear of unauthorized use. During operation the no-fall technology prevents mishaps.

The .45 horsepower, DC motor is designed in the enclosed platform and out of view, so there are no moving parts exposed.

Additional features are available with the Loft-It™. The Deluxe Showcase Enclosure includes tinted polycarbonate transparent panels to protect and offer a 'display case' look for your favorite motorcycle or other items. Two Bike Stands attach to the base frame of the platform for stable bike storage. The Utility Enclosure, translucent side panels, hides the contents from site.

The Loft-It™ Storage Lift System can be professionally installed, and it comes with a one-year limited warranty.

Each **Loft-It™** holds a hefty 1,000 pounds.

All electrical and moving parts are contained beneath the platform.

Cybiag Garage Door Systems, Inc.

7600 West 27th Street, #230

St. Louis Park, MN 55426

Toll-free 877.429.2424   www.GarageScape.com

Garagescape™

Prominence is not always a desirable attribute. That is true especially when the front elevation of a home is dominated by the garage instead of an attractive front entrance.

Garagescape's innovative and patented system provides the method to give your home a facelift. Garage doors are designed to seamlessly match the exterior of the home. Whether your home's exterior is traditional siding, stucco, face brick, stone, or logs, Garagescape's doors take on the appearance of your home. You can add windows, doors, and trim to the garage doors for effect and function.

What may appear to be a quiet cottage in the county… …is an innovative way to improve the appearance of the garage.

There are design requirements. The system works best for single door openings. A minimum 18" clearance is required from the top of the door opening and the ceiling or joists. A minimum of 12" on one side of the interior door is needed to mount the opener.

Usually, a contractor or builder must be hired to apply the finishing exterior materials. An authorized and trained installer comes on site to install the tilt and lifting devices and to the standard door springs and tracks.

Call the telephone number above to learn more about having a Garagescape™ system installed in your home.

This new Victorian was built on a 40'-wide lot limiting the options for a two-car garage.

Harding Steel, Inc. Parking Systems

1751 Gilpin Street, Denver, CO 80218-1205

Toll-free 800.PARK-DBL (727.5325)   www.HardingSteel.com

Car Lift for Residential Garages

You might think car lifts are strictly for the rich and famous. Here's an example that could change your mind. This car lift proved to be a practical solution for a special situation.

A couple owned a lot in the historic district of town. They planned to build a new Victorian-style home. Most lot sizes in neighborhoods of this vintage were narrow—their lot was only 40' wide. This width limit prohibited them from building a two-car garage on the front of the home. According to city code, they could build a one-car garage in front and run a driveway along the side to the backyard where they could build a detached two-car garage. Most home owners would have agreed to that design.

But the couple had plans for the backyard that did not include a garage. They did not like the inconvenience or the distance of a detached garage away from the home. For example—carrying groceries during bad weather into the house.

Their plans included an expansive deck for entertaining. They envisioned a koi pond and water feature. In time, they would fulfill a dream of building a greenhouse. The proposed detached garage would eliminate those plans.

The high-tech Car Lift belies the Victorian design, but the advantages have been proven to these home owners.

By employing some innovative thinking, they decided on installing a lift in a single-car garage. After talking to their builder, it was determined that the lift could be built to accommodate two cars. The cost of the lift was commensurate with the cost of building a second bay in the garage. But the result enabled them a place to park both cars, and achieve full use their backyard.

The heavy-duty steel car lift was installed in two days. The lift operates by key switch for safety rea-

Their plans included an expansive deck for entertaining. They envisioned a koi pond and water feature. In time, they would fulfill a dream of building a greenhouse. The proposed detached garage would eliminate those plans.

sons. The two-piston hydraulic power unit is very quiet—almost totally silent.

The house was designed around the tallest point in the garage. The ingenuity to include the car lift solved several problems. The front elevation of the home was spared from having a garage prominence, which would have been uncharacteristic for their home's architectural style.

Hovair Systems Inc.,

6912 South 220th Street, Kent, WA 98032

800.237.4518/Office 253.872.0405   www.hovair.com

Hovair Systems Vehicle Turntable

Maneuvering your car into a tight spot in the driveway or garage can be cumbersome and always troublesome. The vehicle turntable exists as a viable option to turn your life around toward a convenient solution for turning your car around. Even if the opportunity were available to buy adjacent real estate to widen the driveway, the vehicle turntable proves to be a financially competitive alternative.

The air-bearing technology is the operative principle for the vehicle turntable. The low-profile design operates on a thin layer of air to move tons of steel in the exact location you desire. A shallow pit of just 4" to 5" is all that is required to install the Hovair turntable. The rotation operates manually or automatically. And you can choose to operate the system from a panel-mounted location or use a remote control.

The Hovair turntable can be installed outside or inside. One home owner in Southern California has a subterranean garage which offered no turning space. The tight radius and steep driveway approach made it nearly impossible to consider backing out of the garage. He installed the Hovair turntable and recommends this solution to others.

Another example included a Hovair turntable installed in Florida that serves double duty. In addition to directing the car in pinpoint fashion inside the spacious garage, this home owner uses the turntable as a revolving stage for musical performances to entertain friends.

This highly specialized system is designed by engineers. The company entertains serious inquiries only, so if you have been looking for a solution to turn things around, the good folks at Hovair Systems are prepared to help.

Oriental Flowers

Feng Shui is the relationship between people
and their home and work environments.
Applying Feng Shui principles of design and
placement promote good energy or ch'i
resulting in harmony, prosperity, and fulfillment.

FENG SHUI FOR THE GARAGE:
Practical applications
for everyday living Gary Hendrickson, Assoc., AIA

If the key words for real estate are "location, location, location," then the key words in Feng Shui are "entrance, entrance, entrance!" I'm speaking about the architecturally-planned main door—your Grand Entrance!

Most houses are built with attached garages, and we drive into our garages and wade through the obstacle course of garden tools, sports equipment, stacks of newspaper, paint cans, etc., on the way into our houses. If we're lucky, we don't trip and fall face first into the laundry room.

Welcome to the modern world. Our journey into our home wasn't always like this, however. In the old days, there was the *ming tang* to enter before getting to the main front door—a beautiful garden with a walkway meandering from the street to the front door of the home. The *ming tang* defined a transition point from the outer world to your inner sanctum, your place of rejuvenation, inspiration and reconnection—your home, your temple.

In the busy world outside of your home, your thoughts revolved around the day's business, tomorrow's errands or next month's special ceremony. The *ming tang* provided a moment to exit the outer, busy world before you entered your home where your focus shifts to the matters of the family.

Today, the main entry into most homes is the garage door—primarily because of convenience and security. It's easier and quicker to carry groceries directly into the kitchen from the garage; and once you pull into your garage, the door closes; you are home safe and sound.

Unfortunately, for most homes, the *ming tang* doesn't exist. Today's Grand Entrance is an expanse of concrete and a boring, thin, garage door.

If the garage door is your grand entrance, I'm sorry to say that it does not serve to soothe your soul. You are impacted emotionally, spiritually and physically by the first impression of what you see as soon as you drive into your garage. This negative impact works on both the subconscious and physical levels. And it grows worse if you are tripping over the clutter along the pathway from your car to the door to your home.

Without a calm, peaceful entryway, our sense of place and honor of ourselves is successfully—though unconsciously—diminished.

Clutter and disorganization in the garage represent a form of stuck energy. When you realize that, you are ready to enter the realm of Feng Shui, the ancient Asian science and art of placement and design. Feng Shui is used as the basis for designing new buildings or for

A modern-day example of **ming tang**.

enhancing existing ones. When used in a business or in a home, Feng Shui fosters health, harmony and prosperity. During the last decade, Feng Shui has become so popular in the West that it has been featured in mainstream magazines, newspapers, and on TV shows around the world. Well-known developers, multinational corporations, individuals, and businesses worldwide are now seeking help from Feng Shui experts.

Clutter and disorganization in the garage represent a form of stuck energy.
When you realize that, you are ready to enter the realm of Feng Shui...

There are many techniques or schools of Feng Shui. For this book, I'll simplify by explaining the most familiar concerns and by providing some common solutions. I will focus on one very popular style known as the Black Hat Sect School, which uses the Bagua (fig. 1) or eight-sided octagon-shaped diagram overlaid on the floor plan of the house.

In this Feng Shui cosmology, nine equal-sized areas are dispersed throughout the house. Each area represents various aspects of life known as *Life Stations*. If you divide your house into equal thirds in each direction, like a tic-tac-toe diagram, you have eight perimeter areas plus the center area. These are called the nine areas of the Bagua. Although most often illustrated as an octagon, it is easier to simply draw a rectangle grid over the floor plan.

The goal of this analysis is to observe where each of these areas are located in your house plan, and to assess whether each of these *Life Stations* are flowing smoothly in your life.

Using the front door to orient the Bagua, some of the front three sectors often spill over partially into the garage (fig. 2).

Knowledge, career, and helpful people are those areas that most often occupy the garage in the typical American house floor plan. If any of these areas need a boost in your life, you can elevate those areas to the level of importance by placing pictures, inspirational passages, sculptures, beautiful collages, posters, affirmations, photos, or other decorative and meaningful elements in these locations to bring out or remind you of the qualities or goals that you desire in your life.

Bagua areas can be impacted by symbology

The goal of this analysis is to observe where each of these areas are located in your house plan, and to assess whether each of these Life Stations are flowing smoothly in your life.

and intent. Since manifesting your goals is influenced by the degree of your desire and passion for what you want, be clear about the importance of the area to your life. Ask yourself: "How much do I really want to make changes in this *specific* area of my life?"

If these areas of the Bagua are filled with clutter or broken items, that is a reflection of that area of your life! If your garage is disorganized and contains most or all of the *helpful people* or *benefactors'* area, you may be experiencing difficulty in maintaining reliable relationships with colleagues, assistants or helpful friends.

If the Bagua areas of *career* and/or *knowledge* are mostly in your disorganized garage, you might be out of work, experience limited success if you're self-employed, seeking a direction if you are between jobs, or feel a lack of recognition and respect in your current position.

Clean up, organize and decorate your garage. Then watch what happens to those corresponding Bagua areas of your life!

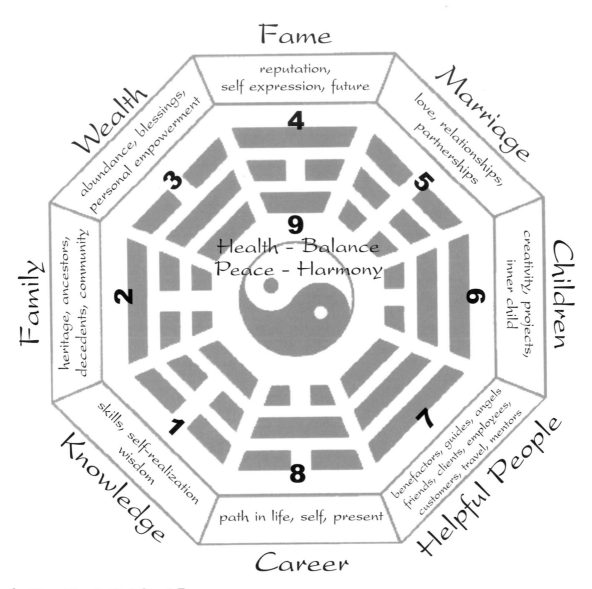

Fig. 1 - The Black Hat Sect Bagua
These numbers shown in the Bagua are for corresponding references only for the house plans cited in this chapter.

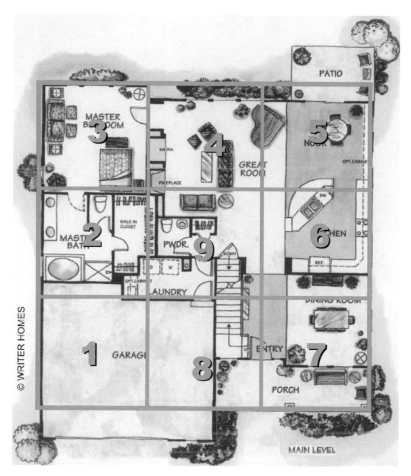

Fig. 2

Here are some commonly asked questions:

Q: How do I overlay the Bagua over the house plan with a garage? Do I include the garage in the Bagua or not?

A: The Bagua Life Station areas represent aspects of your everyday life experience within the main living areas of the house. The garage activities mostly include parking the cars, storage, and occasional crafts or handyman tasks. Therefore, the garage represents only a small allocation of time and can be deleted from the main house energy Bagua grid. (fig. 3).

Exceptions to this guideline are when other rooms on the floor plan surround or are placed behind the garage, or when the second-floor plan places rooms over the garage.

Q: How do I place the Bagua grid over the floor plan if the garage partially protrudes into the main area of the house?

A: This condition is shown in figure 2. Using the 'rule of 1/2' if the majority of the horizontal distance across the main living area of the house is greater than the horizontal distance across the garage, then draw the Bagua grid across the inside wall line at the front of the house and continue through the garage to the inside of the exterior wall of the garage. Part of the garage will be inside the various areas of the Bagua, leaving the rest of the garage area to be extensions beyond the grid.

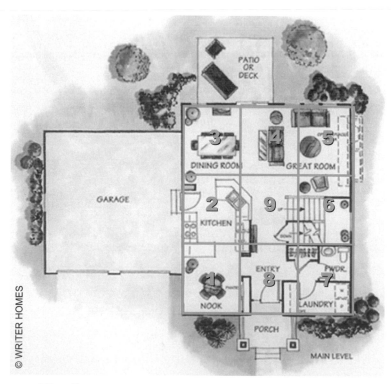

Fig. 3

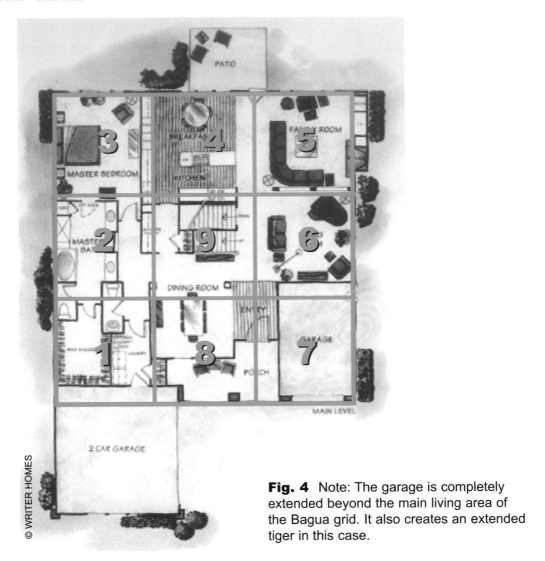

Fig. 4 Note: The garage is completely extended beyond the main living area of the Bagua grid. It also creates an extended tiger in this case.

When the garage projects horizontally more than half the distance of the length of the house, then draw the Bagua grid line across the inside of the front of the garage wall to the opposite side of the house's exterior wall. This creates what is called a 'missing area.' There is no missing area when the garage is the only part extended completely beyond the front of the house or if the garage faces a different direction from the front of the house (fig. 4).

Another subtle influence on our lives is the Feng Shui concept called the Dragon and the Tiger. Looking out from your front door, the Dragon is on your left and the Tiger is on your right. In landscape Feng Shui, known as the Form School, the Dragon represents male energy and the Tiger represents female energy. Garages protruding out from the front of the house create extended Dragons or Tigers (fig. 4). This could contribute to a slightly noticeable imbalance between the primary male and female living in the house, possibly leading to authority or power struggles. If the resident is single, this could reflect difficulty attracting the opposite sex. One solution for this is to increase relationship intentions in the appropriate areas of the house and master bedroom with symbology representing your desires or goals for that area of your life. You could place a sculpture or other item at the corner of the missing area to remind yourself of your goals or feelings you wish to embrace.

Q: Are colors and lighting important for the garage?

A: The garage is usually a much cluttered yin space. Create more balance for the space by bringing in yang energy. First, bring in more reflective lighting that covers floor space and add task-oriented lighting. Secondly, paint the walls and floor in light colors. Metal colors are best for brightening up a garage area. Colors include shades of light grays and off-whites. These colors are available for specialized garage-floor coatings.

Q: What does my workbench have to do with Feng Shui?

A: Workbench areas are notorious areas for clutter. Feng Shui philosophy suggests a cluttered space represents a cluttered mind. By stripping away the clutter and organizing the surface area, you'll utilize this most important principle in Feng Shui design. And you'll be able to find that socket wrench just when you need it! Remember, create a home for everything.

Q: Where should I install cabinets?

A: Taller built-ins and storage cabinets that appear bulkier should be placed close to the division wall between the garage and the house. Smaller or more open cabinets and racks should be installed closer to the garage doors. These basic guidelines use the *Form School* of energy flow for support and comfort in any space.

Other Feng Shui issues and concerns

Many Feng Shui authors and practitioners complain that garages contribute to "bad" Feng Shui for various reasons:

1. Toxic smells and odors from garages waft throughout the house can cause physical and mental illnesses. Eliminate the odor source. Upon implementing the recommendations from this book, you'll discover that an organized garage is also much easier to clean, thus, the source of odors vanishes leaving no opportunity for these situations to occur.

2. The garage is historically an uninteresting, disorganized, ugly, dirty, clutter-and-dust-collecting space, filled with fumes and grime that are not suitable

for living space. Previously, there was not much incentive to keep it neat and clean. Once again, transforming your garage into a functional and multipurpose space gives hope to adding positive energy to a space formerly ignored. Home owners get more use from their garages through implementing innovative ideas. They discover a peaceful and ever-inspiring entry upon arriving home in a clean and organized garage.

3. Bedrooms over garages are problems. Large spaces located under bedrooms are busy with cars coming and going. If you have this type of house design, determine if you can add more insulation to create a sound barrier. If practical, choose to use a bedroom over the garage as an office or guest room. If you're designing a new home, it would be advisable to avoid locating bedrooms over the garage.

These Feng Shui techniques that I have provided present a different perspective and yet support the principles in this book. Have fun with remodeling and organizing your garage. May your life be filled with beautifully organized environments that bring you much abundance, peace, prosperity, and health!

A media room over the garage like this house by Trendmaker Homes in Houston, Texas, is a good alternative to a bedroom over the garage.

Gary Hendrickson, *Assoc. AIA, is a nationally known Feng Shui instructor, author, lecturer, consultant, and home and office designer for 27 years. He is the managing director for Feng Shui Design International in Boulder, Colorado. His popular 'Weaving the Web' course series is taught throughout the country. Gary is a Founding Council Member of the International Feng Shui Guild and a member of the American Society of Feng Shui. He is presently writing a book, Feng Shui Full Circle.*

He can be reached at 1.877.728.9149

www.fengshuidesign.net

or his e-mail at info@fengshuidesign.net

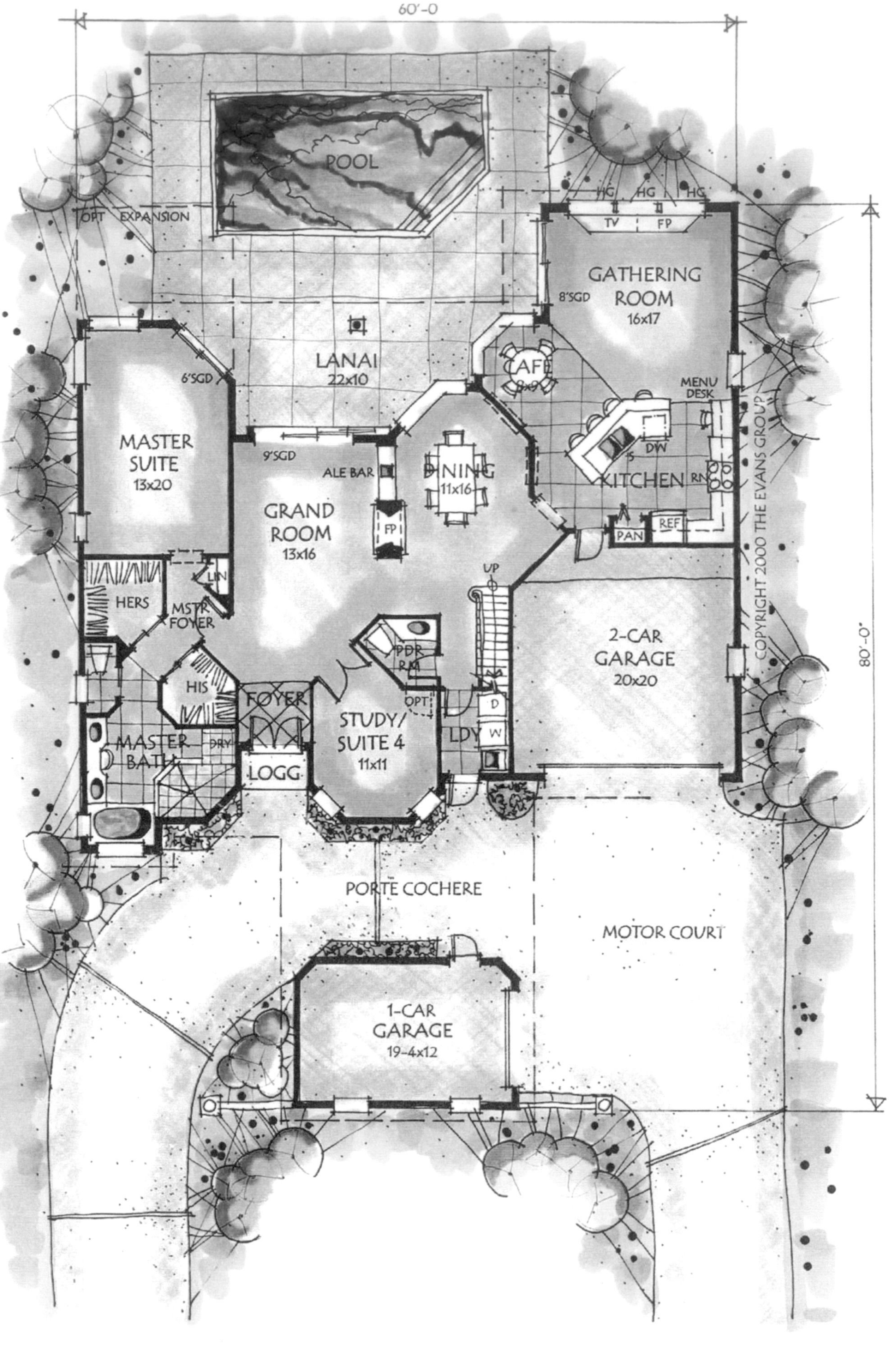

60'-0

POOL

OPT EXPANSION

HG HG HG

TV FP

GATHERING ROOM
16x17

8'SGD

LANAI
22x10

MENU DESK

CAF

6'SGD

MASTER SUITE
13x20

9'SGD

ALE BAR

DINING
11x16

KITCHEN

DW

FP

GRAND ROOM
13x16

RN

PAN REF

LIN

HERS

MSTR FOYER

UP

2-CAR GARAGE
20x20

HIS

FOYER

PDR RM

STUDY/ SUITE 4
11x11

OPT

D

W

LDY

MASTER BATH

DRY

LOGG

80'-0"

PORTE COCHERE

MOTOR COURT

1-CAR GARAGE
19-4x12

COPYRIGHT 2000 THE EVANS GROUP

ARCHITECTURAL DESIGN CONCEPTS FOR THE GARAGE WHEN BUILDING A NEW HOME

A new home requires months and sometimes years to plan and design. The details are immense. If you are planning to build, be sure to invest time with the garage design as it relates to the overall architectural scheme of the house.

I interviewed three veteran architects to learn how their design concepts that illustrate how innovative ideas incorporate garage design and how they enhance the appearance of a new home.

All house plans and designs featured here are owned and copyrighted by the respective architects.

Scenario I. The disappearing garage doors

Floor plan #1

Drive around many neighborhoods and it's apparent the garage looms as a bulbous appendage on the front elevations of houses. This can be avoided with good home design. A design by architect Don Evans from Orlando, Florida, eliminates this problem.

The design below reveals a driveway leading through a porte cochere to the attached two-car garage positioned toward the back of the house. A sports court bordered by three sides of

Floor plan 1

Within the floor plan:

Hers
Master Bathing
His
knee space

Master Suite
20-2 x 14
Sitting

HIGH GLASS

railing
opt. s.g.d.

Deck
18 x 19

2 Car Garage
20 x 20

Den/ Guest
13 x 12

Verandah
18 x 27

up Optional

Lined Lined f.p. t.v.

Leisure Room
15-10 x 14

RAIL

Ldy.

Friends Foyer

42" HT. COUNTER

Sports Court
32 x 28

Back Porch

Cafe
10 x 10

Kitchen

buffet niche

Dining
13 x 12

DECO CLG.

Suite 3
12 x 11

SOFFIT ABV.

BEAM ABV.

Play Toy Garage
12 x 20

Porte Cochere
13 x 17-6

Bath

Int. ridge

Parlor
16 x 14
vol. clg.

HIGH GLASS

plant shelf abv.

ARCH

Suite 2
14 x 11

Foyer

Front Porch
9 x 8

FLOOR PLAN

the home adds privacy and security. The sports court creates space that can be used for a variety of activities not normally undertaken on a driveway that is located adjacent to the street.

In this design, a third garage bay known as the play/toy garage, provides suitable storage for that vintage car, motorcycle, and other "toys." Small children may discover this to be a fun playroom; and it's a perfect place for birthday parties. The sports court provides plenty of space for children's games, too.

The dimensions of the driveway — 32' X 28' — provide a generous space in which to maneuver turnarounds while backing from the two-car garage.

Note the location of the play/toy garage on the front elevation. It appears that this garage is a part of the home. The absence of garage doors emphasizes the design elements of the house. It suggests also that less visual invasion projected by garage doors creates more focus and interest in the home.

Floor plan #2

This floor plan illustrates a five-car garage. The visual impact is diminished because the garage utilizes back-to-back design to stack cars in rows. Unless the household is blessed with several teen-agers of driving age, most families do not own five cars. But many families need big garages to house boats, classic cars, RVs, and other adult toys.

In this floor plan, the garage is designed for the front of the home. Even though the garage is about 36' X 30', it is integrated architecturally, and the front elevation of the home is attractive.

Mr. Evans insists that lot size does not need to be a limiting factor in producing a design that accommodates a large garage and an attractive house. A lot size measuring 50' X 135' can accommodate a multi-car garage. Focus first on what you want. These plans for mansions or mini-mansions can be scaled down. And what's learned from those designs can be used in production homes. The use of sports courts and porte cocheres are examples.

Floor plan #3

This six-car garage is a large 30' X 50' and located toward the back and side of the home. But who can tell? The porte cochere employs a single-lane driveway. A trellis above the entry of the sports court and well-placed landscaping to the left of the driveway limits any visual impact.

Mr. Evans is quick to point out that "if you have to look at your garage door, you're doing something wrong."

While family size of the typical American household has decreased

"... if you have to look at your garage door, you're doing something wrong."

by 20% in one generation, our homes have grown by 50%! And garage space continues to expand. Architects are more challenged than ever to satisfy esthetics with good design techniques as a result of this growing trend. Mr. Evans offers those solutions.

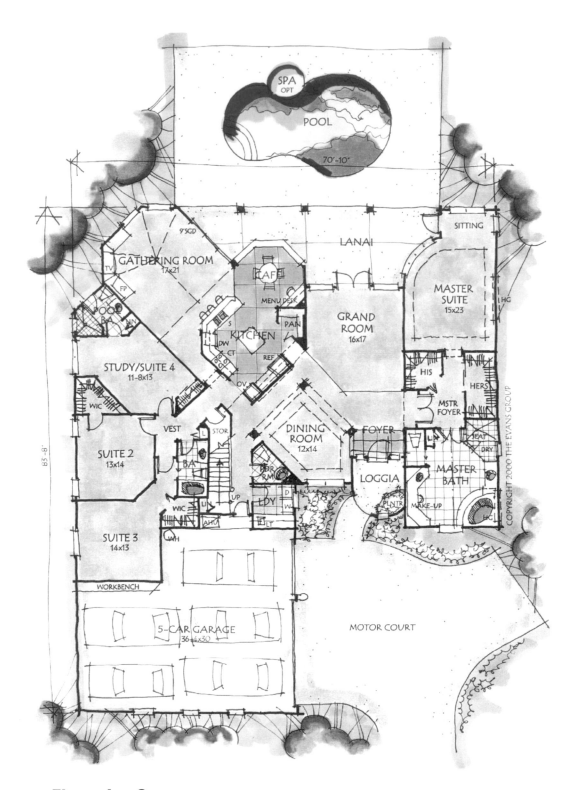

Floor plan 2

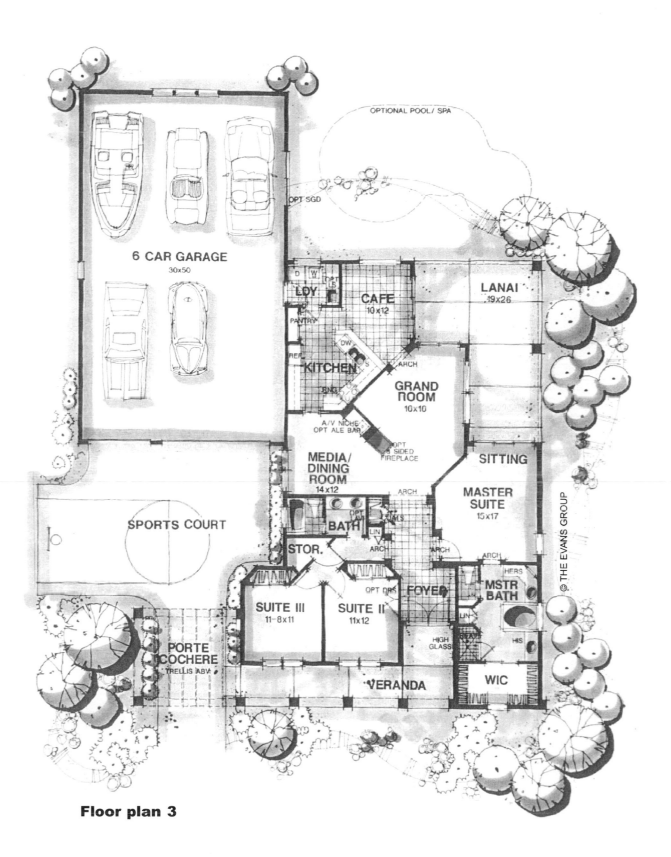

OPTIONAL POOL/ SPA

OPT SGD

6 CAR GARAGE
30x50

LDY

CAFE
10 x12

LANAI
19x26

PANTRY

REF

KITCHEN

DW

RNG

GRAND
ROOM
10x10

ARCH

A/V NICHE
OPT ALE BAR

OPT
3 SIDED
FIREPLACE

MEDIA/
DINING
ROOM
14 x12

SITTING

ARCH

MASTER
SUITE
15 x17

BATH

ARCH

ARCH

SPORTS COURT

STOR.

ARCH

ARCH

MSTR
BATH

HERS

FOYER

OPT DRS

HIGH
GLASS

HIS

SUITE III
11-8 x11

SUITE II
11x12

PORTE
COCHERE
TRELLIS ABV.

VERANDA

WIC

© THE EVANS GROUP

Floor plan 3

Scenario II. 'Flex' space promotes garage functionality

Architect Barry Berkus from Santa Barbara, California, enriches garage space by making it flexible. Flexible, multi-use, multipurpose, or any number of adjectives describes his futuristic 1997 'Home of the Future,' designed for a joint project sponsored by *BUILDER* and *Home* magazines. Flexibility is the design theme for this futuristic home built in Coppell, Texas. But the garage plan is the focus here.

The attractive driveway, which leads to the motor court, provides a sense of space that 'you have arrived.' The motor court doubles as an outdoor recreational area. An overhead trellis is located in front of the motor court, and it spans the width helping to define the space. The trellis also serves as an interesting design element.

Garage doubles as a basketball court.

Home of the future, 1997
Coppell, Texas

PHOTO BY LYNN SUGARMAN

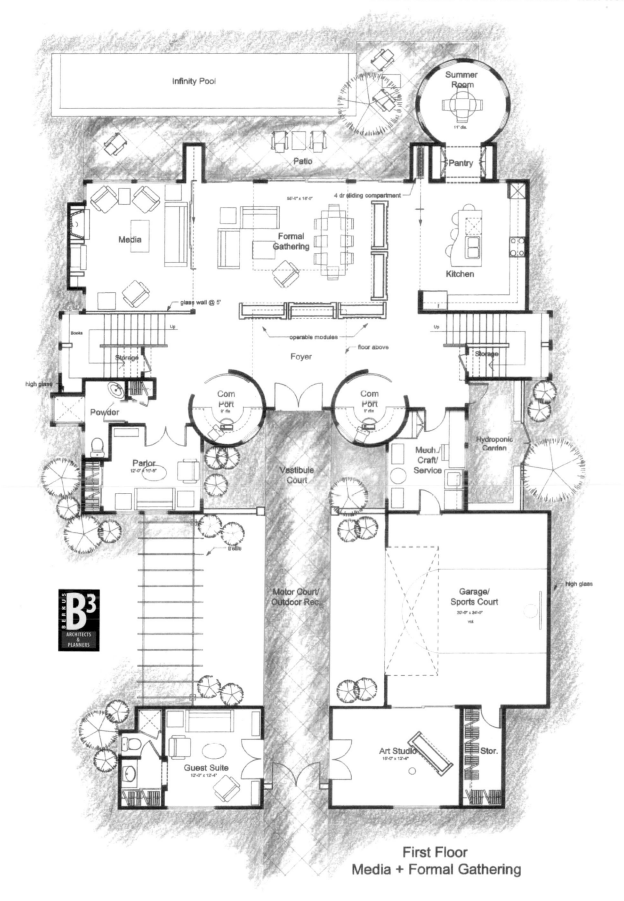

First Floor
Media + Formal Gathering

The entire garage door features panes of contact-resistant glass windows designed to withstand the impact of an errant basketball. When the garage door is open, the motor court and garage interior space combine to create an expansive area that is perfect for kids' sports or parties.

The garage floor space is 20' X 24'. The ceiling height is 21'. Lines are painted on the garage floor for half-court basketball, and the basketball standard is located on the wall. You can play tennis or roller hockey inside this garage. On the wall opposite the garage door, a row of windows located near the ceiling provides additional light.

The floor plan includes a transition room that serves multiple purposes. It is the laundry room, storage for cleaning supplies, has a large sink for cleanups, a recycling center, and counter space for backpacks and groceries.

Because the garage is designed to be used for many activities, a separate, adjacent room is designed for most storage needs. Another adjacent room is designed as a get-away room suitable for an art studio or workshop. Private spaces exist throughout the home that foster the theme of flexibility, allowing the home owners and future owners to use and define space based on their needs.

"This home is about creating memorable family events."

"This home is all about creating memorable family events," Mr. Berkus said of his design. Thanks to his ideas, homes of the future will hold plenty of 'flex' space.

Scenario III. Class 'A' motorhome poses garage design challenge

What's 38' long, weighs six tons, and needs a garage? A motorhome, of course. This mobile behemoth presented a special design challenge to be solved by architect Anton M. Dattilo from Austin, Texas. He had completed a home design for clients when they announced they had purchased a class 'A' motorhome— it needed a home too! With a sharp eye for design and a freshly sharpened drawing pencil, Mr. Dattilo designed a garage for the motorhome without sacrificing the overall appearance of the home. (See Fig. 1)

You may never acquire a class 'A' motorhome, but it's possible that you may acquire a cabin cruiser, an RV, or some other oversized conveyance that requires inside storage. So how can you achieve the objective without sacrificing good design?

With some innovative thinking, Mr. Dattilo was able to create a compatible home design even for the family motorhome. Here's what he did. He had topography in his favor because the land sloped away from the garage. A retaining wall had to be erected along the slope that separated the original detached two-car garage. (See Fig. 2) Had the lot been level, extensive and expensive excavation would have been required to lower the profile of the garage for the motorhome.

Fig. 1

The detached two-car garage was connected to the main house with a covered walkway that provided an integrated design. The garage bay for the motorhome extended in back. Mr. Dattilo artfully created a courtyard effect in back of the garage to provide visual appeal from the backyard. This was important not only for the sake of the home owners' day-to-day living, but for creating an overall scheme for backyard entertaining.

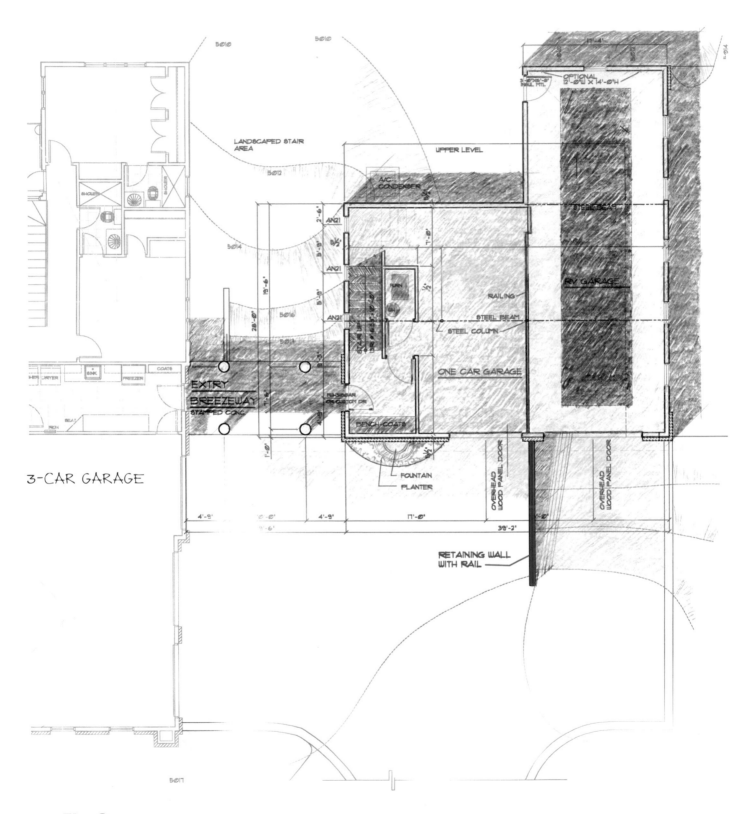

3-CAR GARAGE

Fig. 2

Profiles of the contributing architects

Donald F. Evans, AIA

Mr. Evans is Founder and President of The Evans Group and is headquartered in Orlando, Florida. He was awarded the 1988 Professional Achievement Award for Architecture from *Professional Builder* magazine for his leadership in housing innovation. He is a featured speaker at major industry events. He is an active member of the American Institute of Architects, National Association of Home Builders, and the Urban Land Institute.

1001 North Orange Avenue
Orlando, Florida 32801
407.650.8770
www.TheEvansGroup.com

Barry A. Berkus, AIA

Founder of B3 Architects and Berkus Design Studio in Santa Barbara, California, he has been recognized as one of the world's leading architects by *Architectural Digest*. *Professional Builder* magazine honored him as the most innovative architect in the area of housing in the United States. *Builder* magazine cited him as being among the 100 most influential individuals in the past century in American housing.

2020 Alameda Padre Serra, Suite 133
Santa Barbara, California 93103
805.966.1547
www.BerkusDesignStudio.com

Anton M. Dattilo

Mr. Dattilo specializes in custom home design. He has offices in Colorado and Texas. He resides in Texas and has been a professional architect since 1978.

8329 Lofty Lane
Round Rock, Texas 78681
512.341.2221
http://home.att.net/~amdarchitect

INTERIOR FEATURE IDEAS FOR THE GARAGE WHEN REMODELING OR BUILDING A NEW HOME

Here are some ideas for the garage that can save money before you start to remodel or build a new home and garage. With a little forethought you'll gain more use and enjoyment from your garage later.

How many times have you said: "I should have done *that* when I was building our home." You're not alone.

Insulate garage walls and ceiling

No matter the climate, insulation protects any structure from the heat and the cold. By installing insulation you'll also gain year-around enjoyment in the garage.

© PHOTO BY RUSSELL LEE

Courtesy of the Library of Congress

Walls and ceiling that are common to interior living space and the garage are required to be insulated by building code. But it's also easy to add insulation to exterior walls.

Installing fiber glass, batt insulation requires only a staple gun.

The 3 1/2" thickness of batt insulation should be attached to the 2" X 4" studs with the paper side visible. The paper serves as a moisture barrier which lessens the risk for mold. This provides an R-13 value. If you have 2" X 6" stud walls, install R-19 batt insulation to take advantage of better insulating properties over the R-13 value.

Garage walls that are drywalled may not always be insulated. Look at the base of the drywall on or near the garage floor - sometimes bits of insulation are evident. To be sure, take an insulated-handled screwdriver and poke a hole in an inconspicuous location on the wall. In the event an electrical wire is pierced, you're protected. Make a larger hole if needed, and with a flashlight look to see if insulation is present.

When no insulation exists, foam insulation can be sprayed into the cavities between the stud walls. Boring a hole in the drywall between each stud near the ceiling enables the foam insulation to conform to the shape of the cavity.

Use slow-curing foam insulation. It is designed to flow over obstructions before it expands and cures.

Foam insulation products are more costly than other types of insulation. But they control air infiltration most effectively.

If attic space exists, blow in fiber glass insulation to at least an R-30 value and preferably to an R-38 value.

Insulate garage doors

Garage door manufacturers make insulation panels to be inserted in the sections of their overhead doors. Home builders often use a basic, garage door model without insulation. Contact the local representative for your garage door manufacturer to determine if insulating the garage door is desirable.

Be sure to check the weather seal around the perimeter of the garage door too. It should be secure to keep out the weather. Also check the seal on the bottom of the door. An arched, vinyl bubble seal works well as a replacement if the existing seal is ineffective.

Open shelving offers versatility for objects of various shapes and sizes. Larger items can be tucked under a shelf on the floor and out of the way.

Built-in open shelving

Designating space for built-in open shelving defines an area for storage. Sometimes open shelving is preferred to closed cabinets and pantries. Open shelving provides storage flexibility for objects of various sizes and shapes. Remember, storage needs change. In addition to cabinets and pantries, open shelving provides storage versatility.

Here's an illustration of an open-shelving assembly. This system is bolted to the wall. The design limits the number of floor support posts or stiles that could interfere with storing items on the shelves. Items such as children's bikes, exercise equipment, etc. that are on the floor can be tucked under the shelves.

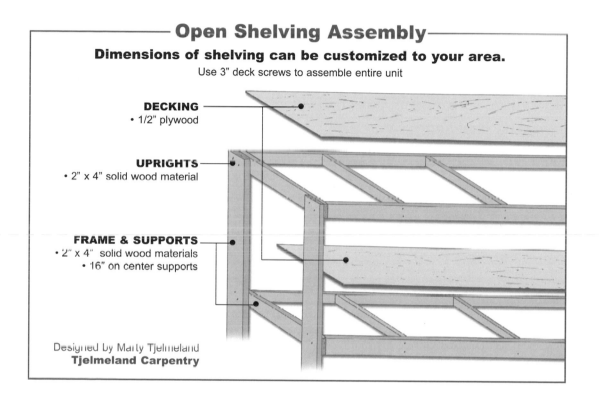

Open Shelving Assembly

Dimensions of shelving can be customized to your area.

Use 3" deck screws to assemble entire unit

DECKING
• 1/2" plywood

UPRIGHTS
• 2" x 4" solid wood material

FRAME & SUPPORTS
• 2" x 4" solid wood materials
• 16" on center supports

Designed by Marly Tjelmeland
Tjelmeland Carpentry

Hot/Cold water supply

Installing a water source in the garage is convenient. Many garages share a common wall with the laundry. In this case, a direct water line can be installed easily when the home is constructed.

But water supply placement is limited due to the proximity of the water source. Planning, therefore, becomes important because other features must be designed around the hot/cold water supply. A retrofit is simple too. You may want to use freeze-proof sillcocks for an unheated garage.

Electrical wiring

Whether you're remodeling or planning your electrical walk-through with a builder for your new home, think about power requirements. Customarily, electrical outlets seem remote from where power is needed.

The double duplex receptacle provides four outlets instead of the standard two-outlet type. The cost is insignificant, so install several of these outlets in strategic areas of the garage conforming to code. Garage space is large in many homes today, so include more outlets for convenience. As you plan about the location for a workbench, include several outlets to accommodate use for a variety of power tools.

It's a good idea for the circuit to be staggered so that alternating outlets are connected to different circuit breakers. If several power tools are being used for a project, they tend to be plugged into two or three outlets on the same circuit breaker. Alternating these outlets avoids that problem. Also consider installing a 20-amp power instead of 15 amp power for 110 outlets. This provides more power to each outlet. If a lot of power equipment is used, consider 220 outlets with 30-amp power. This will give you confidence to run most power tools plus a sizable air compressor.

Be sure to use a licensed electrician to perform electrical upgrades.

If you like the idea of a television connection in the garage, think about the location that affords the best viewing spot.

A telephone jack is important too. How often does your phone ring inside the home while you're in the garage? Locating it in the garage near the door entering the house makes sense.

Radiant heat doesn't blow dust; it heats objects.

Heating & cooling the garage

If you live in a climate that persistently tallies 110°F day after day, then it is likely the only time you'll use the garage is very early in the morning and at night after the searing temperature subsides. The concept of creating a functional garage is the ability to use it!

Check with a local, licensed HVAC company. It may be possible to tap into the existing air conditioning system for the garage. Air conditioning ducting from inside the house along with a return air vent is required. A fire damper is required to be installed between the living area and garage. If the existing cooling unit is not adequate, a smaller, independent cooling unit can be installed. So for whatever you love doing in the garage, you can do it in cool comfort.

Detroit Radiant Products Co.

21400 Hoover Road, Warren, MI 48089

Office 586.756.0950   www.Reverberray.com

Radiant heating is commonly used in commercial and industrial buildings. The garage is also a suitable location for several reasons:

- Radiant heat warms objects and not just the air.

- This type of heat is more effective and quicker than forced-air heating options.

- Hot air blowing in a garage can cause a swirl of dirt or sawdust which can be aggravating. Imagine painting or varnishing with dust blowing on your freshly painted veneer.

- Radiant heat is absorbed by the floors and re-radiated into the air.

- Radiant heat is more efficient than other options, saving approximately 10%-20% in energy costs for a residential garage.

Follow manufacturer's instructions to optimize the benefits of radiant heating.

The Re-Verber-Ray tube heater consists of three components: a control/burner box, radiant tubing and reflectors. Detroit Radiant's LD Series is the appropriate model for garage heating.

Ceiling installation should be at least 8 1/2' from the garage floor. The manufacturer recommends ceiling installation against a wall. This allows heat to be dispersed throughout the garage. Overhead installation is permissible, but the heat can be direct and too intense. Give some thought to the best location for installation because you know best where you need the heat. Outside ventilation is required. A licensed heating and air conditioning company is required to install this system. Their professional advice can guide the installation process.

Consider these ideas too:

- For efficiency, consider installing a digital thermostat.
- Master on/off switch prohibits needless heating.
- Do not place combustible material within four feet of the radiant heater.
- If the garage floor is coated with an oil-based epoxy, it might emit a foul odor where radiant heating is installed.

The Re-Verber-Ray heating system is available in 10' to 30' lengths with 5' extensions. The manufacturer recommends the maximum length not exceed 30'.

BONUS IDEAS:
Going beyond the garage

Here are a few garage-inspired ideas that work well in other areas of the home and outside the home.

Laundry, Basement, Closets

The wall organizing systems explained on pages 39-46 can be adapted for other areas in the home. Here are some examples:

- Small suitcases and travel bags hang on the wall in our basement storage area.

- Place commonly used tools on a wall organizer so they are easy to find when someone needs to perform a task in the basement.

- My wife installed a wall-organizing system behind the closet door in the master bedroom. Her fashion accessories such as belts, scarves, and purses hang neatly out of the way, and they are easily seen when she needs them.

- Laundry rooms are often underutilized. Use wall organizers to easily expand storage space.

Use a wall organizer in the master bedroom closet.

• Designate spots for coats and hats for each member of the family. Our growing son moves the hook for his coats every year to accommodate bigger sizes.

• Wall organizers accommodate rods which can be used for hanging clothes. This is especially helpful for clothes that wrinkle easily. The rod makes laundry day a bit more tolerable. The rod can be moved to make room for other hanging needs.

Here's a wall with an organizing system that otherwise would be unused space.

Outside: Beautify the garage with floral hanging baskets

Hanging baskets beneath the eave in front of garage doors softens the front elevation of the house. But remembering to water the baskets can be a problem especially if the flowers are exposed to late-day sunshine. They bake.

If you have an automatic sprinkler system, expansion kits are available to set up automatic watering for hanging baskets. Expansion kits come with micro tubing, 1/4" clamp holders, inline shutoffs, and emitters. If these kits are not in stock, these items can be purchased separately at nurseries, sprinkler companies, or most hardware stores.

Here's how to do it:

Connect micro tubing into the system on the side of the house that is closest to the garage. If possible, connect to the station that waters the flowers and shrubs. Make sure the tubing is long enough after installation to cover the length to the last hanging basket.

Run the microtubes along the eaves behind the fascia as shown.

The drip system works to refresh your flowers all summer.

Installations tips:

- Run the micro tubing on the side of the garage up to the eave that overhangs the garage.
- Attach the tubing with 1/4" clamp holders as the tubing is being installed.
- Run the tubing along the length of the eave against the exposed, bottom portion of the fascia board on the house side. This is the main line.
- Cut more micro tubing lines into the proper lengths to reach each basket from the main line. These are the feed lines.
- With a 'T' connector, insert the feed lines into the main line. Use the 1/4" clamps connecting the feed lines under the eave toward the house. These feedlines should be long enough to reach each basket.
- Insert an inline shutoff on the end of each feed line.
- Attach the emitter to the shutoff for each feed line.

Test the system. Be sure that each inline shutoff is in 'off' position. Naturally, turn on the station connecting the newly installed watering system. Begin with the last hanging basket to receive water, and gently open the inline shutoff. Then open the other shutoffs until water is flowing to each basket.

While lawns do not require watering each day, flower beds, shrubs, and trees must be watered more often. A separate program on the sprinkler clock for flowers, shrubs, and trees helps to conserve water. You do not need to run the entire system.

Not all sprinkler systems can accommodate add-ons. Where water pressure is weak, not all plants may receive an adequate amount of water. If you are unsure, contact a representative from a reliable sprinkler company.

Garage Annex

I am often asked about what to do with large equipment that takes up a lot of floor space such as the lawn mower, wheelbarrow, tiller, snow blower, etc. Sometimes designating space for them in the garage is your only option. Another option is to add a garage annex. The annex is an enclosed shed added to the side of the garage to store large equipment.

Before starting construction, check with local authorities to determine building permit requirements. Setback rules established by cities dictate the distance that any improvement can be from the side lot line. Some municipalities may not require a building permit depending on the overall size and height for the annex. Subdivisions that have active home owners' associations may have architectural control guidelines requiring approval before any addition or remodeling can occur. These authorities may determine the size of an annex or if it can be built.

The size of an annex should be based on your storage needs. For example, the outside dimensions may be only 5' x 10'. This provides 50 square feet of floor storage for large equipment. Measure your large equipment to determine the floor area needed. This is the basis to determine the size of the annex. Build the annex so that it is architecturally compatible with the house. If possible, construct it 10' tall. This provides lots of interior volume for potential storage. Additionally, the walls and ceiling become available for tool storage. All the lawn and garden supplies can be stored here. The annex is an ideal winter home for patio furniture, the umbrellas, and the gas grill.

The recommended door location is on one end of the annex. This creates ideal interior wall space for storing longer items such as ladders or patio umbrellas. If a door is positioned on the longer wall, it needlessly wastes interior wall space.

To download a free set of plans for the garage annex, go online to www.Garagez.com. This 10-page set of plans can be used to obtain a building permit if one is required. It can be useful to present to the architectural committee for its review. All specifications are included with the free download. 🏠

Visually, the garage annex addition blends architecturally with the house.

The cubic volume in the garage annex provides sizable storage space for lawn and garden supplies and equipment.

FAMOUS GARAGES:
The incubator of American industry

The genesis of the garage occurred when Henry Ford invented the Quadracycle in 1896 in his coal shed. Doors in the shed weren't large enough to allow Ford to remove his new invention and give it a test drive. So he pounded an opening in the brick wall large enough to escape the confines of the dusty shed and motored down the lane. Little did he know that he was inadvertently inventing the garage! Since then, the garage has played the role of incubator for other American entrepreneurs for more than 100 years.

Hewlett-Packard Company

William R. Hewlett and David Packard spawned the high-tech industry on the West Coast in 1938 in Hewlett's 12' X 18' garage adjacent to his rented home in Palo Alto, California. With $538 in capital, their work in the garage marked the beginning of what is now the Hewlett-Packard Co.

This garage with the rented home became Hewlett-Packard's first "Corporate Headquarters."

Photo courtesy of Donald Laird's California State Historic Landmarks   www.calandmarks.com

Their first product was the audio oscillator. Their first order came from The Walt Disney Company.

Dr. Frederick Terman, a Stanford University professor, encouraged his students to start their own electronics companies instead of heading to East Coast companies. Hewlett and Packard took the advice seriously.

The home and garage on Addison Avenue is a registered historical landmark in California. This modest structure is considered to be the "Birthplace of Silicon Valley."

© DANIEL G. ROTHSCHILD, circa 1977

© DISNEY ENTERPRISES, INC.

Imagine a young Walt Disney setting up his camera to begin creating animation in his uncle's garage in 1923.

The Walt Disney Company

Moving from the Midwest to Hollywood in 1923, Walt Disney moved into his Uncle Robert's home. Disney struggled to make ends meet. His desire to become a producer faded as his money dwindled. At his uncle's urging, Disney set up a camera stand in the garage to create animation. Fortunately, Disney took his uncle's advice!

In October of that year, he received news that a New York distributor was interested in several of Disney's cartoon series. October 16, 1923, marked the beginning of The Walt Disney Company when a contract was signed with the distributor.

He soon outgrew the garage in Los Angeles, and he moved a few blocks away where he rented the back half of a real estate office to establish his studio.

Disney was fond of saying, "I only hope that we never lose sight of one thing—that it was all started by a mouse," as he reflected later on his company's humble beginnings.

Well, it may have been started by a mouse, but it began in the garage!

PHOTO BY VAUGHN HYSINGER

Apple Computer started in 1976 in this modest Los Altos, California garage.

Apple Computer

At age 12, Steve Jobs called Bill Hewlett to discuss a project Jobs was working on. It wasn't the personal computer, but after a 20-minute conversation, Jobs had the parts for his project and a promise of a summer job at Hewlett-Packard.

Jobs later became acquainted with Stephen Wozniak. Their paths crossed from time to time during their younger years. Later, Wozniak became an engineer at Hewlett-Packard. Jobs was employed at Atari. In his spare time, Wozniak was building a personal computer, and he and Jobs started collaborating. Their respective companies did not believe the computer industry would ever serve individuals; so their employers declined to consider the project proposed by the two whiz kids.

In 1976, the two visionaries started Apple Computer in the Jobs' family garage in Los Altos, California. An old, wooden bench served as the assembly station for computers to be built. The garage soon became Apple's manufacturing plant and shipping department.

Buddy Holly

Even Rock 'n Roll can trace its early roots to the family garage where Buddy Holly and his band practiced in Lubbock, Texas, in the mid to late '50s.

While the Holley family lived in several rented homes in Lubbock, the home pictured here was their place of residence in 1957. That was the year when Holly's hit song, "That'll Be the Day" became the best selling record in the country.

Garage bands flourished in the '60s with resurgence in their popu-

PHOTO BY BOB CROSIER

Imagine hearing the music coming from this garage in Lubbock, Texas on hot summer nights.

larity in the '80s. While few of these bands achieved fame, seldom were they a 'hit' with the neighbors. Many neighborhoods today have restrictive and protective covenants that are enforceable. Garage bands are not specifically prohibited, but their noise might be.

For the first few years PING® putters were made at Karsten and Louise Solheim's garage.

Karsten Solheim with PING® putter.
circa: 1959

Karsten Manufacturing

The widely-heralded Ping® 1A putter was invented by Karsten Solheim in his Redwood City, California garage in the late '50s and patented in 1959. The putter's moniker came from the sound made when the putter hit the ball.

Solheim was a mechanical engineer for General Electric. His avocation was inventing and manufacturing golf clubs during his free time. He used sand casting for molding the clubs' heads. He determined that hiring a company to perform the tooling on the club heads would be too expensive. So he found a used milling machine for sale for $1,100 which he purchased with borrowed money. That was the only money he borrowed to launch the company.

Of course, the milling machine was set up in the family garage. He had no tooling experience, but that served as no deterrent. After work, he spent countless hours working on each putter and crafting them to perfection.

In late summer of 1959, *Sports Illustrated* treated the 1A putter as a novelty and labeled it the 'musical putter.' As a result of the publicity, an East Coast company ordered 100 putters which it used for Christmas gifts. That sent manufacturing into full swing. Solheim's dinner hour was often delayed as the club head was heat-treated on the burners of the stove top.

Solheim's professional duties with GE required him to commute often to the Phoenix area. This reduced his time for manufacturing. So in 1961, he persuaded GE to transfer him to Arizona. His family bought a house on several acres with a large garage which enabled him to continue manufacturing the golf clubs.

PHOTO BY BRUCE WYCKOFF

The PING® 1A putter was invented in this Redwood City, California garage.

Several professional players in 1965 at the World Cup, an international golf tournament in Japan used the Ping® putter. The event was televised, and following that telecast, orders grew dramatically. He continued to manufacture the putter in the garage until Karsten Manufacturing moved to a north Phoenix location in 1967. The headquarters are still located there.

Imprinted on all putters is the name of the city where they are manufactured. An early vintage Redwood City Ping® 1A putter sells easily today for around $2,000. One putter sold at auction for a whopping $20,000! The original retail price for the 1A model was just $17.50.

Motown - Hitsville USA

The two-family flat on West Grand Boulevard in Detroit was the home of Berry Gordy, Jr. and his family. The songwriter bought the home in 1959. The family lived upstairs and Berry's Motown Recording Corporation operated downstairs. The dining room table served as the 'shipping department' during the early days. Mr. Gordy's dream was to record music and manage singers. "Hitsville USA" was born.

The garage was converted into Studio A and included a control room and recording equipment. Long before the invention of synthesizers and digital recording, the Motown "echo chamber" produced stunning reverberation effects for recording. The chamber, however, was nothing more than a hole cut in the ceiling.

Studio A was open 24 hours a day from 1959 to 1972. The artists continued to record there even after the Motown Recording Corporation moved into its new headquarters in a 10-story office building in downtown Detroit in 1968.

Imagine Diana Ross and the Supremes, Stevie Wonder, Smokey Robinson and the Miracles, the Temptations, Four Tops, Gladys Knight and the Pips, and so many more famous groups got their starts in a garage!

This famous garage is now open to the public. You can visit the Motown Historical Museum, and see it just as it was when it started in 1959.

A. T. PRESCOTT.

DOOR AND OPERATING MECHANISM THEREFOR.

APPLICATION FILED APR. 10, 1916.

1,273,923.

Patented July 30, 1918.

5 SHEETS—SHEET 1.

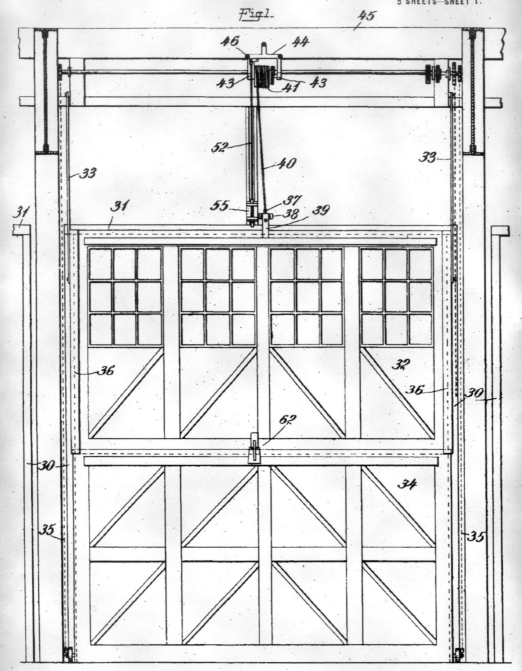

Fig1.

Inventor

Arthur T. Prescott

By his Attorney

E. W. Marshall

GARAGE TRIVIA

Here are a few tidbits of garage trivia that might come in handy at your next cocktail party when there is a lull in the conversation and everyone is waiting for the last batch of Swedish meatballs to simmer in the fondue pot.

The HP trophy garage

In September 2000, the Hewlett-Packard Company bought the garage where the company was founded in 1938 for a whopping $1.7 million. The Palo Alto property included a modest detached house for no additional charge.

Conspicuous construction

Microsoft's Bill and Melinda Gates have garage space to accommodate 17 cars in their new $56 million compound near Seattle. The 66,000 square-foot mansion includes 52 miles of communication cable enabling the couple to remotely program lighting, music, temperature control, and even draw a bath to a prescribed temperature!

God's garage

Nicknamed "God's Garage," Pope John Paul II blessed the newly-built Vatican garage which is large enough for 91 buses and 723 cars. The top floor features a coffee bar, a 430-seat cafeteria, a restaurant and shops. Bill Gate's, eat your heart out.

The wonderful garage of Disney

Walt Disney got his start in his Uncle Robert Disney's garage in North Hollywood in 1923. The garage was saved from demolition in 1984 by the Garden Grove Historical Society. They moved the garage to the Stanley Ranch Museum in Garden Grove.

© DANIEL G. ROTHSCHILD, circa 1977

There's no garage today at this Kingswell address in Los Angeles.

An EPA nightmare

During the early days of the automobile there were no gas stations. So how did drivers fill the gas tank? Automobile owners installed underground gas tanks in or near their garages. A bulk gasoline truck would keep the home owners supplied with gasoline, and the home owner would operate a hand crank pump to nourish the car with fuel when needed. Imagine the Environmental Protection Agency attempting to monitor all of those underground tanks today.

Ladies and gentlemen, Elvis has left the garage

According to a Graceland spokesman, Elvis converted Graceland's four-car garage into an apartment in 1960. He preferred to display his shiny Cadillacs "all out front, ready to go."

From horses to horsepower

William Howard Taft served as the 27th President from 1909-1913, and he is the first U. S. President to own a car. He converted the horse stables at the White House into a four-car garage.

He said what?

The phrase "a chicken in every pot" was coined by presidential hopeful Herbert Hoover as he campaigned for the 1928 election. He promised also "a car in every garage." He won the election, but he could not deliver on his promises as the nation's economy went to pot in 1929.

Better call MAACO™

The cost to repaint a large car in the 1920s was over $500. And repainting had to occur yearly if the car was parked outside. This gave birth to the development of commercial parking garages.

Commercial radio got its start in the garage

Westinghouse Electric engineer Frank Conrad began broadcasting from his Pittsburgh garage in 1919 after spending nights and weekends tinkering in the garage behind his home and started radio station 8XK. He teamed up with a local record store providing on-air endorsements in exchange for records to be played continuously. Westinghouse Electric seized the commercial opportunities of radio and started KDKA in 1920.

When was the automatic garage door opener invented?

Upon the conclusion of a television interview for this book, the camera man asked what was the most significant innovation in the garage during the 20th century. Caught off guard, I offered a lame reply — the three-car garage. But as he dismantled his camera equipment, he suggested that it was the invention of the automatic door opener. Of course, he was correct.

The Overhead Garage Door Company lays claim to their founder C. G. Johnson as the individual who invented the upward-lifting garage door in 1921. He is also credited by company history as being the first inventor of the electric door opener in 1926. The Overhead Garage Door Company is certainly the first and longest, sustaining residential door opener company in America, and it would appear there were others who patented garage door openers even though some openers were powered by various means.

According to reports discovered in an old trade magazine of the forerunner association to the International Door Association, R. N. Flack and L. D. Sturn were granted a patent for an electric garage door opener June 29, 1926; they then formed the Automatic Door Device Co. in Portland, Ore. In announcing the company's formation, the inventors proclaimed in company literature that: "The demands of the automobile public for luxuries being so great, the idea for a device to open and close (the) garage door by electricity has caused us to perfect this device…the result has been even more successful than we expected."

...what was the most significant innovation in the garage during the 20th century?

Further research was required.

Popular Mechanics in 1922 in the 'Amateur Mechanics' column featured a new patent for an opener. But the story failed to acknowledge the inventor. The article states, "The device was operated with a motor mounted on the ceiling of the garage, which opened and closed the bi-fold doors while the motor's operation was controlled by a

---

The automobile would drive over a vertically-positioned lever in the driveway triggering an intricate system to open the garage door.

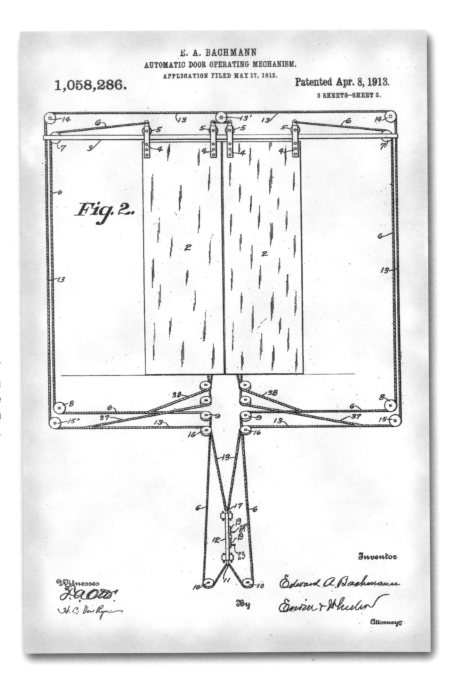

spring-mounted plate in the driveway which, when driven over by a car, threw a switch…While it would keep ne'er-do-wells from rifling through the garage, it would not keep someone from backing a truck up to the door and emptying the (contents of the) garage."

Another similar, automatic door opener that included a treadle in the driveway and powered with a hydraulic mechanism was invented in 1916 by Slvanus B. Roy of Massachusetts.

As early as 1913, a patent was granted to Edward A. Bachmann from Wisconsin, whose invention was called an automatic door-operating mechanism even though it was not electrically powered. The device opened the garage door upon the automobile driving over a lever positioned vertically. The lever was connected to a myriad of cables fashioned around an intricate series of 18 pulleys.

Much credit is given to the ingenuity of these inventors who developed various types of the early automatic garage door openers, but the economic viability beyond the point of earning a patent is in question. Other inventors, to their credit, earned patents for garage door openers, but to say with absolute certitude who first invented the automatic door opener is difficult to ascertain.

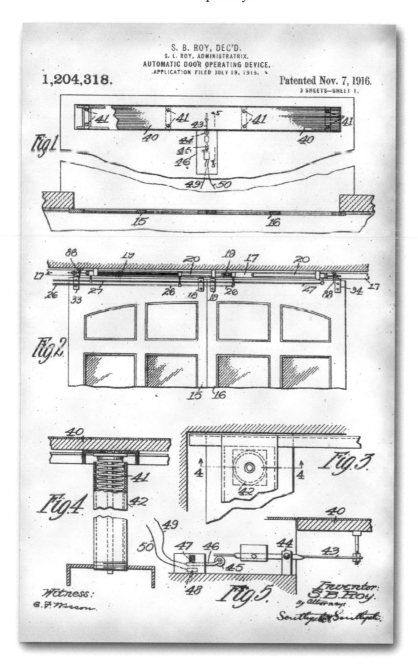

This automatic door opener from 1916 worked when the automobile drove over a treadle in the driveway activating a hydraulic mechanism to open the garage door.

"The garage feature of our modern home environment has attained the point of permanency…Its contribution to the home atmosphere is surely worthy of more consideration than the neglect or indifference that appears to be the attitude of so many home owners."

—Dorothy and Julian Olney
The American Home Book of Garages, **1931**

A CENTURY OF HISTORICAL TRENDS IN THE GARAGE

TREND I - The detached garage: 1910-1930

Garages were exceedingly rare during the first decade of the 20th century. The automobiles were housed in a converted coal or tool shed; some automobiles cohabitated with horses in the carriage house or with other farm animals in the barn.

Most garages were detached from the home because the 'newfangled' automobile posed a fire threat to the home owner. Many automobiles caught fire frequently and because filling stations were virtually nonexistent, the home owner resorted to underground gasoline tanks in the garage, carriage house, or barn.

In 1910, only 458,000 automobiles were registered in the United States. A decade later the number increased to 8,132,000.[1]

The advent of the assembly line in 1914 by Henry Ford doubled the output for manufacturing automobiles, and the cost was cut in half providing for an expanding market.[2] While the cost of the automobile was within the reach of the middle class, only the wealthy could afford to build garages and many garages were designed by architects. Many early garages for the wealthy class were constructed in masonry or stucco because of the fire hazard. Insurance companies disapproved of garages built of framed construction.[3]

1 Jackson, Kenneth T., *Crabgrass Frontier: The Suburbanization of the United States*, p. 161, Oxford University Press, NY, 1985.
2 Dent, Harry S., *The Roaring 2000s*, p. 67, Simon & Schuster, NY, 1998.
3 Comstock, Wm. Phillips, *Garages and Motor Boat Houses*, p. 5, The William T. Comstock Co., NY, 1911.

TREND II - The attached one-car garage: 1930-1965

Detached garages continued to be built in the 1930s, but another choice for construction evolved that eventually became the norm for new homes.

The National Automobile Chamber of Commerce reported in 1930 that the number of registered automobiles had risen from 3,200 to 23,121,589 in 30 years. The automobile was built safer without the fear attached of it becoming an inferno on four wheels. In 1927, building codes adopted construction standards that included firewalls between the home and the garage.[4] Authors of an early book about garages written in 1931 had this to say about attached garages becoming a trend: "To the prospective home owner these days it seems to be somewhat of a problem whether he shall have the usual form of detached garage or one which is attached to the house. The trend now appears to be definitely toward the latter form…Twenty years ago it probably never occurred to anyone they would ever be otherwise. But the automobile is now a vastly improved vehicle and old prejudices and dangers have been removed…The prevailing building codes, however, now include regulations which provide ample security against the fire hazard when the car is housed in the dwelling itself."[5]

In 1910, only 458,000 automobiles were registered in the United States. A decade later the number increased to 8,132,000.

The desire for convenience and safety when the family exited the automobile into the home anytime night or day from the attached garage created a sought-after feature in housing construction that continues today. The attached garage became a permanent fixture for the most part in housing, but middle-class families possessed the needed one-car garage. Attached, one-car garages were prevalent for more than 30 years. The Depression years of the '30s stifled the economy and resulted in the lowest rate of home ownership—43.6% by 1940–during the 20th century.[6] World War II affected the psyche of a nation for most of 20 years. The economic times prolonged this trend for 35 years.

---

4 California Real Estate Inspection Association, Internet, 2000.
5 Olney, Dorothy and Julian, *The American Home Book of Garages*, p. 10-11, Doubleday, Doran & Company, Inc., NY, 1931.
6 U. S. Census Bureau, *Historical Census of Housing Tables- Homeownership*.

TREND III - The automatic garage door opener: 1954-1979

One device that once was seen as a luxury item is a necessity today: the garage door opener. The Alliance Manufacturing Co. purchased the garage door opener from U. S. Motors, and it conducted a brief merchandising experiment. Soon after, in 1954 the Alliance "Genie" was the first mass-produced, radio-controlled residential garage door opener.[7]

Large, expensive homes installed the garage door opener; it was not until the late 1970s that it became a widespread trend. Discovering a home today without a garage door opener in just about any price range is indeed rare. But it took 25 years for this trend to become established.

TREND IV - The two-car garage: 1968-1991

"Motor car manufacturers look forward confidently to the time when every family will have two, if not three, cars"

—Lewis Mumford, 1958, Architectural critic, philosopher, urban planner

Mr. Mumford's words were prophetic. Families of the post-World War II generation included children who demanded to drive at age 16. Car sales soared throughout the '60s. The late 1960s was robust with virtually full employment giving a sense of new prosperity to prospective home owners. This affluence enabled them to buy the latest features and upgrades, and one emerging trend was that of the attached, two-car garage.

The building of suburbs spawned the demand for two-car families perhaps more than any other factor. Families had to drive farther distances for basic services, to work, and to transport family members to various activities. Suburbia transformed the American way of life as families fled heavily-populated cities. Today, with the revitalization of many major American cities, there is a growing desire for living in these downtown centers. Among the empty nesters, this raises a reasonable question: Will families continue to own two cars? Count on it.

Two car garages dominated home construction over homes built with only a one-car garage by two to one. But by the end of the '70s that ratio rose to 7:1, and that same relationship remained steady throughout the 1980s

A sense of independence and individualism permeated America throughout the 1960s. The Women's Movement sparked a renewed freedom among many women, even those living in traditional families. They expressed their new-found independence by embarking on new careers, or at the very least obtaining a job that enabled them to add a new dimension to their identity. They required transportation, and parking their car overnight in the driveway was not acceptable.

---

7 Overhead Door Corporation, website

More women entered the work force in the 1970s not necessarily because of a feminist philosophy, but due to a sluggish economy in the first half of the decade. Two incomes were needed to support a household. Add the commencement of an inflationary economy in the latter half of the '70s, and the two-income family was well-ensconced as a cultural norm due to rising prices placing pressure on the family budget. Rising prices were accentuated in most housing markets throughout America relative to other consumable and durable goods, so the rush for housing was on before escalating prices locked out prospective and move-up home owners. Most home buyers stretch their housing dollar to obtain the features desired, and to that end, the attached, two-car garage became the mainstay in the majority of new homes constructed.

Two car garages dominated home construction over homes built with only a one-car garage by two to one. But by the end of the '70s that ratio rose to 7:1, and that same relationship remained steady throughout the 1980s.[8]

It is clear those societal norms, economic factors, urban planning and population demographics converged creating the need to include the attached, two-car garage to newly built homes. In 1989, 70% of the homes built had two-car garages. Only 10% of the homes built had a one-car garage. But in the late 1980s, a budding, new concept was being introduced to new-home construction: the three-car garage.

TREND V - The three-car garage: the benchmark year is 1992

In 1980, the National Association of Home Builders conducted a survey to determine if home owners wanted three-car garages. Less than a quarter of the respondents preferred a three-car garage. A 1985 survey gave similar results. But in 1995, the survey yielded a 32% affirmative response to include a three-car garage in a home. The desire for more garage space resulted because people accumulated more possessions—not because they were buying more automobiles. Car sales dipped slightly from 15.4 million to 14.8 million units per year in the decade after 1985.[9]

The Characteristics of New Housing compiled by the U. S. Census Bureau, historically cites homes by category for having either a 'one-car garage' or 'two or more garages.' Each annual report included a tabular comparison for the previous four years. *The Characteristics of New Housing* report for 1995 added the 'three cars or more' category for the first time, and in the process, the report for the previous four years was revised beginning with the 1991 report. The statistics were not significant to render the number of homes built with three or more garages. But in 1992, 11% of newly-built homes had 'three or more garages.' For each year thereafter until the end of the decade, the rate of growth remained the same. By 1999, 16% of all new homes had at least a three-car garage. Sixteen percent represents 209,000 of the 1.3

8 U. S. Census Bureau, *Characteristics of New Housing*, 1971-1989
9 Slywotsky, Adrian & Wise, Richard, *How to Grow Markets when Markets Don't*, p. 131, Warner Books Inc., NY, 2003

million homes built in all price ranges for 1999.[10] This is a significant housing trend that is as prominent as the garage on the front of your house.

The price of the home is a determinant as to the garage size. The 1997 housing survey showed that of the homes that sold for $200,000 to $249,999, more than one-quarter were built with at least a three-car garage. For homes that sold for $300,000 or more, slightly more than 50% included at least a three-car garage.[11]

For homes that sold for $300,000 or more, slightly more than 50% included at least a three-car garage.

More interestingly, a 1996 survey by the U. S. Department of Energy revealed that nearly half of home owners possessing at least a three-car garage usually parked only one or *no* cars in their garages![12]

Three car or larger garages barely made a blip on the Census Bureau's radar screen in 1991. But by 1999, 16% of all new homes were built with at least a three-car garage.

10 U. S. Census Bureau, *Characteristics of New Housing*, 1991-1999.
11 Colburn, Andrea, Housing Economics Newsletter, p. 13, *National Association of Home Builders*, September, 1998.
12 Colburn, Andrea, Housing Economics Newsletter, p. 14, *National Association of Home Builders*, September, 1998.

TREND I: DETACHED GARAGE

The garage protected the automobile from the weather. The benefit extended performance and prolonged the automobile's useful life for the owner. The detached garage assured the home's safety in the event the car burst into flames.

TREND II: ATTACHED GARAGE

The automobile became reliable and building codes strengthened. Home owners accepted the attached garage. It meant greater safety and convenience to the family.

TREND III: GARAGE DOOR OPENER

Direct access into the garage provided security and convenience.

TREND IV: TWO-CAR GARAGE

More drivers in the family required more cars and therefore the larger garage.

TREND V: THREE-CAR GARAGE

The third garage bay became popular for the occasional vintage car or family boat. But expanded storage capacity fueled the desire for large garages.

TREND VI: REMODELED & ORGANIZED GARAGE

Home owners in the 21st century leverage garage space by revamping the cluttered garage, reclaiming storage space, and restoring the garage for functional uses.

MY 2020 VISION OF THE GARAGE FOR THE FUTURE

My acuity may not be 20/20, yet I offer some insight about how the Great American Garage will look by the year 2020. The physical characteristics, various uses, and who will be making decisions regarding use are all a part of the make-up of the sixth, major trend in the garage.

Garages are a significant asset for a home. While they will continue to be used as the best place for cars, garages can provide far more utility for your home. Home owners will live longer in their homes, which suggests that they will demand more value in the improvements made in those homes. Part of achieving that value is creating efficient space utilization. By 2020, garage space will be viewed as a fun place, shedding its dismal past as a repository for clutter.

So here are my predictions that will create the sixth, major trend in the Brave New World of Garages in 2020.

Flexible space promotes many activities

The garage is an integrated part of the home utilized by all family members because certain tasks are better relegated to the garage. Crafts, hobbies, science projects, even games are better suited for the garage. And how about these uses: children's birthday parties; Cub Scout den meetings; a guy's hangout for watching television and lifting weights; a place for your youngster's little league baseball team to watch instructional videos during inclement weather. The garage becomes the ultimate, multipurpose room—the home's 'flex' space providing flexible options for various activities. Yes, the garage becomes flexible enough to park cars.

The garage becomes the ultimate, multipurpose room...

Lighting makes the garage more inviting

Great lighting helps create a space that is inviting. Gone are the exposed light bulbs with a ceramic base. No one enjoys spending time in activities in a dimly lit room. Perceptions of the garage as being a dark, dingy, and cluttered area are gone. Upon completion of a garage transformation, those perceptions will be changed, and the lighting will be a pleasant enhancement.

Resilient flooring delivers easy maintenance

The greasy and grimy floor exists no more. Tracking dirt into the house is a distant memory. No longer is the garage viewed as an appendage to the home. Flooring options create an environment that is conducive for activities by all family members.

Companies will continue to develop resilient floor coatings and coverings specifically for the garage that are environmentally safe, easy to apply, and easy to clean and maintain. Floor coatings and coverings change garage futility to garage utility because the sense of space is expanded with lighter-colored floor surfaces. Home owners can be creative with colors and patterns.

Workbench designs integrate ergonomics, form and function

The workbench is a family activity center for hobbies and crafts. A workbench will no longer be a puny four-feet long, but more likely it will be at least eight-feet long to accommodate a variety of projects. Ergonomic designs for the workbench will create a more satisfying experience. No more stooping over a project putting stress on the lower back. Today one national company offers a clear-maple wood work surface that is 1 1/2" thick. The workbench is the furniture for the garage, so design, materials used, and nifty drawers beneath the work surface increase the value of the workbench. The backing above the work surface features shelves and tool racks, but the difference will be the backing is made of the same material as the workbench giving the appearance that the workbench is one, integrated unit.

Removable clamping vises are prevalent rather than the typical, bolted vise. These products are available today, but the removable vise gains in popularity as its utility is recognized to maintain a flexible, work space on the workbench.

Garage interiors incorporate space planning for efficiency

Interior designers create multipurpose space much like kitchens are designed. Standard garage depth is 24 feet to accommodate vehicles and to provide a desirable work space. Twenty-foot depth is the old standard.

Consumers can choose to incorporate an array of options when building a new home such as cabinetry, sports lockers, wet sink, lighting packages, heating and cooling, electrical options, ceiling storage, workbench, wall storage systems, and many more products not yet on the market. An unfinished garage in a new home by 2020 will be rare.

An unfinished garage in a new home by 2020 will be rare.

Temperature-controlled garages create year-around comfort

Climates with extreme temperatures prompt home owners to opt for heating and cooling units for the garage to gain year around usage. Radiant heating systems create a comfortable garage in extreme cold weather regions. Today, nationally known Florida architect, Don Evans incorporates air conditioning in the garages of upscale retirement homes. He refers to these rooms as the "living garage." Garage door manufacturers are improving insulation by making doors with better seals around the perimeter of the door opening. Future advancements will continue as people use the garage more.

Women influence the demand for this emerging trend

Women exert much influence in adapting the multipurpose garage. *Traditional Home* magazine noted in a survey that one out of every three women home owners who have experienced a major remodeling project or built a new home say they were the sole decision maker, and another 40% shared the decisions equally with their partners.

Men and women alike reported that if they could choose what they preferred in a new home, they both would choose an oversized garage. More families want more flexible space, according to the article. People want rooms that can be flexible enough to be used as game rooms or exercise rooms, and prefer space that can provide private retreats. This suggests that the garage could provide one solution to meet many consumer preferences.

Here are more facts that illustrate women's economic impact and their influence in decision making about the home:

... one out every three women home owners who have experienced a major remodeling project or built a new home say they were the sole decision maker ...

- Women have a say in the financial decisions in nearly 70% of households;

- Women comprise 43% of the nation's individuals making over $500,000 per year;

- For women making over $100,000 per year, their brand loyalty is stronger than among men, and women are willing to pay more for superior service;[13]

- According to the Bureau of Labor Statistics, 63% of working-age women are employed;

- By 2010, 60% of the USA's wealth will be controlled by women according to *Business Week* and Gallup research;

- Women are buying 61% of major home improvement products according to *The Wall Street Journal*;

- Women initiate 80% of the purchase decisions when it comes to kitchen cabinets, flooring, and bathrooms according to Forbes Magazine, 2003;

- Women spent 40% of the $187.6 billion for home improvement products in 2001 according to "*Some Women*," 2002.

New home builders respond to the garage design and finish trend

The garage for the future that is created in 2020 occurs because new home builders see the benefits of a clean, functional, and well-organized garage, and those benefits appeal to men and women alike. Various builder options enable the home buyer to create the custom garage suitable to the family's lifestyle.

Architects emphasize design strategies to improve visual appeal

Faced with smaller lot sizes, the visual impact of garages, and the demand for more garage space create the need for innovative designs by architects. New urbanism communities construct the garages on the alley or lane, which inherently produces an appealing front elevation design for the house. The street-oriented subdivision presents more challenge when designing the garage on the front of the home to lessen the visual impact. For example, by incorporating a veranda and a porte cochere on the front of the home and moving the garage to the rear of the home with the addition of a motor court, the home's front elevation is enhanced.

---

13 *Women as an Economic Force*, items 1 through 3, from the Women in Cable & Telecommunications website.

Garage remodeling & organizing enhances the home's value

The finished garage significantly affects a home's value.

Real estate appraisers value a home in the marketplace based on several factors: Buyers' preferences; other similar homes that have sold within a certain time frame; financial market trends; supply and demand of home inventory for both existing and newly constructed homes.

Perceptions of value by home buyers are made based upon expectations of homes in various price ranges. For example, a one-car garage in a $300,000 home would be considered deficient, and the appraiser would make a lower adjustment for the home's value.

As the trend toward functional and finished garages develops, appraisers will consider prospective home buyers' expectations. If a garage is cluttered, disorganized, and void of any storage capacity, and it is a typical garage from the '90s, then a home owner should be prepared for a lower appraised value for that home.

Garage remodeling and organizing: A business opportunity for entrepreneurs

Famous and not-so famous companies started in the garage. Today companies that specialize in garage remodeling and organizing are starting up throughout the country. The heady entrepreneur will seize upon the inevitable emergence of garage remodeling and organizing to provide this service to home owners.

As of 2002, the market for home storage products tallied $800 million in sales. This market will experience double-digit growth as a percentage annually for years to come because of the rising demand to organize and simplify our homes and our lives. Homes are larger, garages are bigger, and almost everyone has more possessions. No one knows how much of the home storage market dollars are allocated to garages. But the garage remodeling and organizing category will grow at such a rapid pace that it will deserve its own market category.

Garage space is typically between 400 and 600 square feet. There are approximately 51.5 million owner-occupied homes with garages. That space and the vast number of garages cannot be ignored by manufacturers. They will tap into the huge demand by developing garage-specific products. Individual garage space is growing larger, and more garages are being built. Not counting rental units, there will be, on average, approximately 500,000 new homes with garages of varying size will be built annually for owner-occupied homes through 2020. And according to the National Association of Realtors, there will be a housing shortage in 2020.

Demographics tell the story: In 2000, about 48% of the population was in the 25 to 59 home-buying age range. In 2020, the percentage drops to 44%, but the overall number of people in the population increases by an estimated 11 million for the range of 25 to 59 year olds.

The growing, affluent senior population group, people 60 to 79, will explode by 170% by 2020 compared to 2000. According to the U. S. Census Bureau, there were 36.3 million people in this age range in 2000, which will grow to 61.6 million people by 2020. According to the American Association of Retired Persons, many in this age group are not retiring, but are 'reinventing' themselves. This suggests their affluence will continue.

There are approximately 51.5 million owner-occupied homes with garages. That space and the vast number of garages cannot be ignored by manufacturers.

These demographics foretell the potential for this emerging market, and explain why start-up company GarageTek, a franchise operation, began operations in 2001. Viewed as the market leader in this new, home-improvement category, GarageTek, appeals to the upscale home owner. Others entering the market: Appliance manufacturer Whirlpool® corporation introduced its Gladiator™ GarageWorks in 2002, which features portable appliances with steel tread-plate design exterior and hefty organizing products. In 2003, the Coleman Company announced plans for its 'Coleman Furniture for Your Garage' by introducing a product line that "features modular flexibility of design and layout, strong steel drawer slides, durable Work Shield™ laminate finishes, innovative wall-mounting systems, and user-friendly features such as task lighting and power access" according to a company press release.

There are sure to be many more national companies that will introduce to the consumer market their versions of product lines for garage organizing systems. Will they find success in this emerging market? That will depend upon the business model and especially the product line distribution. Distribution is the key component as to how these companies will deliver their products to the consumer market. Customer satisfaction must be reckoned with, and the most effective manner to achieve high customer satisfaction is to have local accountability for each installation. Local dealers, distributorships, or franchises will provide that local connection to the home owner. Tackling a complete garage make-over is not an

... according to the National Association of Realtors, there will be a housing shortage in 2020.

off-the-shelf proposition that every home owner will embrace. For this reason, national companies cannot depend only on selling their products in stores. Most major home additions and remodeling projects that are undertaken are best assigned to the professional contractor.

Some home owners will take on the project of remodeling and organizing their garage. But as the population ages, fewer people will want to take on the physical skills of construction.

The best example of the do-it-yourself project that goes awry is the home owner who decides to finish the basement. He may save 40% of the cost of construction, but the unfortunate result is that it *looks* like he saved 40%. Adding value when remodeling a basement suggests that the quality of the workmanship is comparable to the finish of the rest of the home.

Garage finish is not intended to be comparable to the home's interior, but the overall look and appeal is important. So if you possess carpenter skills, go for it and save the labor expense. Short cuts are allowable when finding your way home, but they should be avoided when building or remodeling—even the garage!

Consequently, opportunities are strong for local and regional entrepreneurs to enter the garage remodeling and organizing business.

The essential objectives for success are *a passion for the business, an ability to deliver value to the home owner resulting in high customer satisfaction, an ongoing focus on growth, and identifying the products that meet home owners' needs.* A developed business plan among a myriad of other matters are required that will not be discussed here, but if any one of these essential objectives is missing, there is no need to pursue this business opportunity further.

… objectives for success are a passion for the business, an ability to deliver value to the home owner resulting in high customer satisfaction, an ongoing focus on growth, and identifying the products that meet home owners' needs.

While entrepreneurs are independent by nature, they might consider seeking out other like-minded people in their market area who are considering a garage remodeling and organizing business. By forging alliances, they can leverage resources and keep down costs.

Depending upon the local or regional market, there will be at least one other competitor to emerge on the scene. But when an alliance is created early, the business plan implemented, and the brand established, a strong partnership will provide a competitive advantage.

Another exciting aspect of the garage remodeling and organizing business is to connect with home builders. They will contract with local, regional, and national companies to satisfy their garage design and finish demands. Visit a new subdivision and check out model homes to see what home builders are offering as upgrades. Garage design and finish will soon appear on builders' upgrade lists. Much of new home construction is done by subcontractors, so opportunities will be plentiful for the garage organizing companies desiring to expand their business. A company in a local market that is able to create a "show garage" in a model home will create an added advantage to that company's visibility and ultimately to its growth.

Garage design and finish won't be reserved to those building custom homes. Even builders involved in multi-family construction for condominiums and townhomes will discover that offering garage design and finish will help differentiate their product line of homes. Innovation is what fuels demand.

A company in a local market that is able to create a "show garage" in a model home will create an added advantage to that company's visibility and ultimately to its growth.

Condominiums and some townhome developments cater to the first-time home buyer. Condominiums offer limited storage space, and even today's first-time home owners have amassed many possessions. The most cost-effective approach to achieve greater storage is in the garage. By adding just $2,000 to build more garage storage space, a monthly mortgage payment will increase only $11.99. Clearly, this option for first-time home owners will be perceived as a bargain. Garage design and finish companies who initiate new ideas will prosper.

The most cost-effective approach to achieve greater storage is in the garage

Conclusion

Small businesses are the backbone of the nation's economy but small businesses crumble every day like clay pigeons at a shooting range. While the opportunities appear great for garage remodeling and organizing, make these considerations before starting a company: Develop a business plan; study the local or regional housing market; fully investigate the capital requirements of operating a business; consult with a financial advisor and others whose business acumen you admire; develop the value proposition defining how a home owner will benefit by your services; check your organizing skills for layout and design; discover the availability of products that might be offered; know how much the start-up costs will be; think about who will install the products; is there a skilled labor pool? Preparation is just the beginning.

Owning a successful business with a great reputation that soars like an eagle is far better than being a clay pigeon.

The Tale of the Hundredth Monkey

No longer is there garage evolution: Today, garage design represents a revolution against old, worn-out notions about a part of the home that has been simply overlooked and unrecognized for the potential it possesses. Interest is mounting because there's a recognized desire to organize, simplify, and create functional garage space. While this is a new category in home improvement, make no mistake the trend is emerging. The proof of this claim is made with the story of a monkey as told by Dr. Gwendolyn Galsworth from her book *Visual Systems*.

Koshima is a remote island in the Pacific and home to the macaque monkey (macaca fuscata). These wild monkeys had been the subject of research for decades. The macaques are hunters and gatherers devoting much of their time searching for food. Their daily diet consists of buds, leaves, shoots, bark, and fruits. The routine of collecting and feeding behaviors of the monkeys are passed on to their young through example.

In 1952, a team of scientists were researching the macaque feeding behaviors. As a part of the research, raw sweet potatoes were stacked in various locations on the island of Koshima. As the potatoes lay on the beaches, they become encrusted with sand. Upon the discovery of these savory treats, the monkeys tolerated the gritty sand with each bite of the sweet potato.

Surprisingly, an eighteen-month-old female monkey named Imo carried a sand-laden potato to a nearby stream, and washed the potato before she ate it, thus solving the grit problem. Imo taught this new behavior to her mother and then to her playmates. During the following six years all of the macaque monkeys on the island learned the lesson: Wash sand from potato; eat potato. The scientists marveled at this acquired behavior and how it was taught to the others.

When the findings were reported to the outside world, it commenced a stir within the scientific community. A wild monkey altered her relationship with her physical surroundings through a new behavior that was adopted on her own. The awareness of a need, developing it, learning it, and sharing it with other monkeys, and those monkeys shared by teaching the behavior until the behavior existed among virtually all of the monkeys on the island.

In his book about behavior and consciousness, *Lifetide*, Dr. Lyle Watson writes: "In monkey terms this was a cultural revolution comparable almost to the invention of the wheel."

As extraordinary as this story is, this was not the end. While almost all of the monkeys had adopted this behavior, a few had not, but taking the cue from Dr. Watson, as he suggested, ninety-nine monkeys had adopted the behavior as a way of illustration. Then the hundredth monkey became enlightened and acquired the behavior. But the story does not end here either.

For some inexplicable reason, the behavior 'jumped' to another nearby island with macaque monkeys but without the teaching influence. The behavior jumped again to other islands until all of the islands surrounding Kishoma were filled with monkeys washing the sand from their sweet potatoes before eating them. Even more remarkable, the behavior leaped to the mainland of Japan hundreds of miles away from Kishoma. No monkeys were transferred to other islands throughout the experiments, but the behavior was now a part of the body of consciousness among the macaques.

Over 40 years later, similar discoveries in other parts of the world in other unrelated and unconnected areas substantiate what happened but without a scientific explanation just as it occurred on the island of Kishoma. This phenomenon is called The Hundredth Monkey Principle. Once a critical mass is achieved, this knowledge or behavior becomes a part of the collective thought. Scientists, including Nobel Prize winners, can only confirm the results of the phenomenon through first-hand observation. No other 'logical' explanation could ever be offered.

While the critical mass is yet far away, this trend is just beginning to emerge to a higher order in the reinventing of the Great American Garage. 🏠

Create a Vision for
YOUR
GARAGENOUS
ZONE

member

**Professional organizers enhance
daily life by creating enriching,
efficient, and inviting environments
at home or the workplace.**

GEOGRAPHICAL DIRECTORY OF PROFESSIONAL ORGANIZERS

The desire to get organized is only a concept. Creating a plan of action and its execution implements the structure in which one can be actually organized.

Members of the National Association of Professional Organizers listed in this directory can become your ally and catalyst to help chart the course to attain a clean and organized garage based on the recommendations suggested in this book. Many of these professional organizers are willing to travel to consult with home owners to attain the desired results if one is not listed nearby you. The organizers listed here have organizing skills that reach beyond the confines of the garage, so their skills and services can be beneficial to other areas of the home or workplace.

The National Association of Professional Organizers is an educational association, and its more than 2,000 members are dedicated to

The organizers listed here have organizing skills that reach beyond the confines of the garage, so their skills and services can be beneficial to other areas of the home or workplace.

providing a high level of service to achieve results for their clients. NAPO members are dedicated to achieve continued education, to adopt new skills, and to discover new products that benefit their clients.

The NAPO members listed here include their complete contact information. The author of this book is available for consultation with each of the professional organizers listed here as a resource to them when employed by a home owner.

The National Association of Professional Organizers is *The Organizing Authority.*

ARIZONA

Lynn Hall
Clutter No More, Inc.
Scottsdale, Arizona
Toll Free 800.953.3295
Office 858.485.0410
Fax 858.485.9401
info@clutternomore.com
http://www.clutternomore.com
Areas served: Scottsdale/Greater Phoenix area (Maricopa County)

CALIFORNIA

Breeze Carlile
WindDance, Estate & Residential Organizing & Relocation
San Francisco, California
Office 415.776.5924
breeze@winddanceco.com
http://www.winddanceco.com
Areas served: San Francisco Bay Area, and the counties of Marin, Sonoma, San Mateo. Will travel nationally

Meg Connell
Estate, Corporate, & Residential Organizing
Oakland, California
Office 510.482.5892
meg@theorganizedone.com
http://www.TheOrganizedOne.com
Areas served: The Greater San Francisco Bay Area, will travel nationally

Kevin Hall
Clutter No More,® Inc.
12463 Rancho Bernardo Road, PMB 229
San Diego, California   92128
Toll Free 800.953.3295
Office 858.485.0410
Fax 858.485.9401
info@clutternomore.com
http://www.clutternomore.com
Areas served: San Diego Region, Southern California, Phoenix and Scottsdale, Arizona

Janice Kemmer, President
American Business Organizers, Inc.
Chino, California
Office 877.684.0393 or 909.902.0047
organizing@yahoo.com
http://www.yourorganizer.org
Areas served: From Bakersfield south to the Mexican border, west to the Pacific Ocean, and east to the Nevada border, and Las Vegas, Nevada

Jane Reifer
Clutter Control Organizing Services
Fullerton, California
Toll Free 800.CLUTTER (258.8837)
Office 714.525.3678
Fax 714.441.2355
cluttercontrol@earthlink.net
Areas served: The State of California, especially Los Angeles and Orange Counties

Steven Skidmore
Transformations
23403 Lyons Avenue, #200
Valencia, California 91355
Office 888.434.5772
steve@organizepro.com
http://www.OrganizePro.com
Area served: California

Mikki Lesowitz-Soliday
Divine Order
West Hollywood, California
Office 323.654.4565
Fax 323.654.8455
orgnize@aol.com
http://www.divineorderonline.com
Area served: California

COLORADO

Leann Busch
Leann Busch, Professional Organizer
Broomfield, Colorado
Office 303.464.7597
Mobile 303.817.6142
Fax 303.464.7597
lborganizer@hotmail.com
Area served: Throughout the USA

Tracy Davoust
Organizing Made Simple
Durango, Colorado
Office 970.799.3334 or 970.259.1490
Fax 877.684.7045
tdavoust@yahoo.com
Areas served: Southwest Colorado and Northeast New Mexico

Debra Land
"Imagine This"
Brighton, Colorado
Office 303.654.9821
Mobile 303.514.9730
Fax 303.655.1706
imaginethisco@aol.com
Areas served: Brighton, Broomfield, Superior, Louisville, Lafayette, Firestone, Fredrick, Dacono, Longmont, Erie, Arvada, Niwot, Fort Lupton, Plattville, Johnstown, Thornton, Northglen, Commerce City

Bill Lannan
GARAGES>>>TRANSFORMED!
Denver, Colorado
Office 303.779.3005
Mobile 720.480.1456
bill@wklannan.com
http://www.GaragesTransformed.com
Areas served: Denver and the Metro area

John Lazas
HomeWorks!
31257 Burke Road
Golden, Colorado   80403
Office 303.817.3526
Other 303.642.0987
Fax 303.642.0987
jlazas@homeworksorganizing.com
http://www.homeworksorganizing.com
Areas served: Boulder, Jefferson, and Gilpin counties, and Denver

David Newton
House In Order
1033 22nd Avenue Court
Greeley, Colorado   80631
Office 970.351.8682
Fax 970.356.0131
Newtons@yourhouseinorder.com
http://www.YourHouseInOrder.com
Area served: Northern Colorado (Greeley)

Lisa Sarasohn
Hire Order
Boulder, Colorado
Office & Fax   303.544.0505
lisa@hire-order.com
http://www.hire-order.com
Areas served: Boulder County and the greater Denver area

CONNECTICUT

Cheryl Camacho

Cheryl's Interiors-N-More
15 Sullivan Road
Lisbon, Connecticut   06351
Office 860.376.5869
cherylsinteriors@snet.net
Areas served: New London County,
Groton, Mystic, State of Rhode Island

DISTRICT OF COLUMBIA

Jill Lawrence

Jill-of-all-Trades
Washington D. C.
Office 202.544.5455
Fax 202.544.5455
jilltrades2@aol.com
Areas served: Washington D.C.,
Northern Virginia, Maryland

FLORIDA

Monica Bernhardt

TO-DOers
8301 Cypress Plaza Drive, Suite 204
Jacksonville, Florida   32256
Office 904.386.5662
monica@todoers.com
Area served: Northeast Florida

Diane Hatcher

Timesavers Services
Cooper City, Florida
Office 954.252.7511
Fax 954.252.7511
diane@timesaversusa.com
http://www.timesaversusa.com
Areas served: Dade County, Broward
County, Palm Beach County and
throughout south Florida

Susanne Phelps

Clutter Tamer
Office 954.987.0396
Mobile 954.559.3843
sphelps@one.net
http://www.cluttertamer.net
Areas served: Miami, Fort Lauderdale,
and Southeast Florida

ILLINOIS

Cynthia Ivie

Loose Ends Life & Project
Management, Inc.
683 North Milwaukee
Chicago, Illinois   60622
Office 312.275.4000
Other Phone 773.230.7040
Fax 312.275.4009
civie@looseendsinc.com
http://www.looseendsinc.com
Areas served: Anywhere in the
continental USA

MAINE

Cathy Tetenman

Organizer PLUS
Poland Spring, Maine
Office 207.998.2767
sctet@roadtel.com
Area served: Augusta, Portland,
Lewiston-Auburn, Brunswick and Fryeburg

MARYLAND

Janet L. Hall
OverHall Consulting
Post Office Box 263
Port Republic, Maryland   20676
Office 800.687.3740 or 410.586.9440
janet@overhall.com
http://www.overhall.com
Area served: East Coast

Carol Simmonds
The Clutter Cutters, LLC
P.O. Box 1626, Edgwater, MD 21037
Office 410.266.3664
*Areas served: Annapolis and the
surrounding areas*

Susan G. Romanic, Professional Organizer
"Turning chaos into comfort is my specialty"
Organized! by Romanic
Columbia, Maryland
Office 410.995.0435
OrganizedbySue@aol.com
*Areas served: Baltimore County, Howard
County, Anne Arundel County*

MASSACHUSETTS

Patty Bareford
Wide Open Spaces
Concord, Massachusetts 01742
Office 978.369.8030
Fax 978.369.8030
wideopen.spaces@verizon.net
*Areas served: Boston area, south
New Hampshire, Rhode Island*

Joan Buckley
Natural Order
Plymouth, Massachusetts
Office 508.746.2617 or
Toll-free 877.584.0333
brightstar@adelphia.net
*Areas served: south of Boston and
Cape Cod, southeastern Massachusetts*

MICHIGAN

Mary Dykstra
Within Reach Organizing Services
Grand Rapids, Michigan
Office 616.453.2976
Fax 616.453.2976
mary@withinreach.biz
http://www.withinreach.biz
Areas served: Western Michigan and Chicago

"To develop, lead and promote professional organizers and the organizing industry."

MISSION STATEMENT
National Association of Professional Organizers

MISSOURI

Linda Carey
Linda Carey Professional Organizer
Saint Louis, Missouri
Office 314.725.1575
Mobile 314.724.1571
Fax 314.725.2596
lindacarey@lindacarey.com
http://www.LindaCarey.com
*Areas served: Greater Saint Louis area
and willing to travel*

Sally Wolf
Sally's Organizing Services
Kansas City, Missouri
Office 816.444.7530
sally@sallyorganizing.com
*Areas served: Kansas City metro
area, Lawrence, Topeka, Kansas*

MONTANA

Katherine Atteberry
Mind Over Matter - MOM
1757 Highland Boulevard, #28
Bozeman, Montana   59715-7408
Office 406.587.1607
Fax 406.586.3314
organizer@theglobal.net
*Areas served: surrounding Bozeman
area, southwestern Montana*

NEW JERSEY

Deborah Gussoff
In Order®, Inc.
Montclair, New Jersey
Office 973.744.4835
Fax 973.744.4641
deborah@inorder.com
http://www.inorder.com
*Areas served: New Jersey,
Westchester, and New York City*

NEW YORK

Barbara Brock
A Proper Place
New York, New York
Office 212.755.1017
Fax 212.755.1016
bbrock@nyc.rr.com
*Areas served: New York,
Connecticut, New Jersey*

Patricia Burkhart
How Can I Help You, Inc.
34 Quail Run Drive
Deer Park, New York 11729
Office 631.242.7402
Fax 631.242.7402
peetieb@aol.com
*Areas served: New York, New Jersey,
Connecticut, Pennsylvania, and will travel
nationally and internationally*

Stacey Cohen
in place, inc.
Chappaqua, New York
Office 914.263.4487
Fax 914.238.3367
sbcohen@mindspring.com
Area served: Westchester County

NORTH CAROLINA

Donn Droste
ORGANIZERSCENTRAL, LLC.
Wake Forest, North Carolina
Office 919.426.3877
Other Phone 919.426.3759
organizerscentral@nc.rr.com
Area served: Raleigh

Kristin White del Rosso
Pea Organizing Services, Inc.
1412 B East Boulevard, #187
Charlotte, North Carolina   28203
Office 704.533.3311
Fax 704.344.4455
Kristin@thepea.com
http://www.thepea.com
Areas served: Charlotte, NC and the surrounding areas, Greensboro, Raleigh, Chapel Hill, Durham, and in South Carolina, Columbia, Rock Hill, and Fort Mill

OHIO

Birdie Brennan
Birdie Brennan, Professional Organizer
Commercial Point, Ohio
Office 740.983.1550 or
614.297.1550
Residence 740.983.6742
Fax 740.983.3230
brennan1@myexcel.com
Areas served: Columbus and Central Ohio

PENNSYLVANIA

Leslie Robison
Simple Systems Organizing
Green Lane, Pennsylvania
Office 215.234.0204
Fax 215.234.0248
robisongroup@enter.net
http://www.cluttersmith.com
Area served: Southeastern Pennsylvania

SOUTH CAROLINA

Frank Murphy, President
Inventory Management Systems
2615 Wade Hampton Boulevard
Greenville, South Carolina   29615
Office 864.268.7033
Other Phone 864.616.7071
Fax 864.268.7059
ims@practicalorganization.com
http://www.practicalorganization.com
Areas served: North Carolina, South Carolina, Georgia, Florida, Tennessee

NAPO VALUES

1. *Organizing improves the quality of life.*
2. *Professional organizers make a difference.*
3. *Professional organizers impact change.*

member

TENNESSEE

Mary Pankiewicz
Clutter-free & Organized
Whitesburg, Tennessee
Office 423.581.9460 or 865.607.9460
mary@clutter-free.biz
http://www.clutter-free.biz
Area served: Southeastern USA

Samantha Pointer
Get It Together!
Nashville, Tennessee
Office 615.397.1003
Other phone 615.385.1853
Fax 615.279.8037
getittogethernashville@hotmail.com
http://www.organizingguru.com
Areas served: Middle Tennessee and surrounding areas

TEXAS

Barry J. Izsak*
Arranging It All™
Austin, Texas
Office 512.419.7526
Barry@ArrangingItAll.com
http://www.ArrangingItAll.com
Areas served: Texas, New Mexico, Louisiana
*2003-2004 National President of NAPO

Patricia Withrow
Corsicana, Texas
Office 903.872.4778
Areas served: North Central Texas, Central Texas, Louisiana, Arkansas, Oklahoma

VIRGINIA

Rebecca J. Dameron
SimpliFine
Bent Mountain, Virginia
Office 540.929.4142
rdameron@bellatlantic.net
Areas served: Roanoke and the Roanoke Valley

National Association of Professional Organizers

"The Organizing Authority"

WASHINGTON

Laura Bishop
Eliminate Chaos®, LLC
Post Office Box 13043
Mill Creek, Washington   98082
Office 425.670.2551
Mobile 206.250.7669
Fax 425.671.0336
laura@eliminatechaos.com
http://www.eliminatechaos.com
Areas served: Located in Seattle, will work throughout the USA

Sandee Fahlen
Priorities First
Kirkland, Washington
Office 425.821.0658
Fax 425.820.5650
sandee@prioritiesfirst.com
http://www.prioritiesfirst.com
Areas served: Puget Sound and will travel nationally

Judy Lynn
Consider It Done
P. O. Box 1721
Coupeville, Washington   98239
Office 360.678.0712
consider@whidbey.net
http://www.Consider-itdone.com
Areas served: Seattle area and throughout the USA

Karen Roehl
Life Transformation
Kirkland, Washington
Office 425.814.9621
kroehl@comcast.net
http://www.cluttercoach.org
Areas served: Seattle, Shoreline, Edmonds, Lynnwood, Everett, Mukilteo, Lake Forest Park, Kenmore, Kirkland, Bellevue, Woodinville, Monroe, Renton, Newcastle, Des Moines, Tukwila

Shannon Ronald
Professional Organizer
Post Office Box 5314
Tacoma, Washington   98415
Office 253.627.9797
shannon@wamail.net
Areas served: Tacoma, Olympia, Seattle

Kathryn Walker
Home Neat Home
Post Office Box 713
Edmonds, Washington   98020
Office 206.362.3714
Fax 206.362.3714
Kathryn@homeneathome.com
http://www.HomeNeatHome.com
Areas served: King and Snohomish Counties

Resource Directory

Here are additional sources that you can use for garage or home remodeling. My ongoing research through the years enables me to encounter some useful sources that may be helpful to you. Throughout the book, you have been introduced to a wide variety of products and services with their contact information. If you have a specific question about your garage that has not been addressed, send me an e-mail that is provided below. I'm a resource too! Please be patient. I will respond.

General home improvement

www.Improvenet.com

www.BuildFind.com

www.LetsRenovate.com

www.Homeownernet.com

Garage & home organization/storage

www.TheAccessoriesGroup.com

www.SchulteStorage.com

www.WindquestCo.com

www.OnlineOrganizing.com

www.Organized-Living.com

www.Storage2Systems.com

www.OrganizedLiving.com *25 stores located nationwide*

Garage Plans

Jay Behm has been designing garage plans since 1985. He can be reached from 8am to 5pm Eastern time at 800.210.6776, or send an e-mail at **jayb@BehmDesign.com** .

> ### *Build Your Own Garage Manual*
> Published by National Plan Service USA, Inc.,
> 222 James Street, Bensenville, IL 60106
>
> ### *Great Garages, Sheds & Outdoor Buildings*
> Published by Home Planners, LLC, 3275 West
> Ina Road, Suite 110, Tucson, AZ 85741

Great books to help you get organized

Lighten Up! Free Yourself from Clutter, Michelle Passoff

Organizing from the Inside Out, Julie Morgenstern

Cut the Clutter & Stow the Stuff, edited by Lori Baird

How to Get Organized When You Don't Have the Time, Stephanie Culp

How to Get Organized Without Resorting to Arson, Liz Franklin
 A step-by-step guide to clearing your desk without panic or the use of open flame

Books to inspire and inform

Garage - Reinventing the Place We Park, Kira Obolensky, Taunton Press

Visual Systems - Harnessing the Power of a Visual Workplace
and http://www.visualworkplace.com
Gwendolyn D. Galsworth, Ph.D., American Management Association

Roadside America - the Automobile in Design and Culture
edited by Jan Jennings, Iowa State University Press

The Substance of Style, Virginia Postrel, HarperCollinsPublishers

Share your innovative ideas for future Garagenous Zone® publications

How do you use your garage? What cool and innovative ideas have you included? Share them by sending a description and photographs to the contact information below. Sorry, photographs cannot be returned. By submitting your ideas and photos, you agree to allow them to be featured in future publications or the website. Please indicate if you would prefer to remain anonymous; otherwise, you will be given full credit for your innovative ideas. Information for photo credits should be included.

Garagenous Zone® product reviews

Are you a vendor or manufacturer of a product for the garage that you would like to be reviewed that might be included in future publications or website? Send me a query to the address below before sending any products.

Not all products can be included for publication or appear in the website.

Are you a corporate buyer for innovative products?

Inventors and manufacturers for new and innovative products for the garage are seeking market outlets for distribution. If you are a corporate buyer for your company's catalog, retail stores, or the internet, be on the leading edge to showcase the latest products for the garage. Use the contact information below.

Where have all the famous garages gone?

Are you aware of a famous garage? Many discoveries and inventions that we benefit from or use today are the result of someone tinkering in the garage. That's what makes a garage famous. Someone did something remarkable in the garage.

Send the story and any photos that you are willing to share. Photos cannot be returned. But please include any photo credits. The address and city where the garage is located are essential information. Additional contacts that have a historical perspective for a famous garage would be helpful for further research.

RESOURCE DIRECTORY

ILLUSTRATION BY MICHAEL LINLEY

Look for the latest innovative ideas for the garage at www.Garagez.com

Get Garage Savvy

Contact Bill West to appear at trade shows, grand openings, new-home neighborhoods, conduct seminars, or any special event to add the *sizzle* about this new category in home improvement.

Paragon Garage Company, Ltd.

1324 Paragon Place

Fort Collins, Colorado 80525-9126

Toll-free 866.8GARAGE (842.7243)

Direct 970.223.0505

Facsimile 970.207.1002

bwest@ParagonGarage.com

About the Author

Bill West wrote the book *Your Garagenous Zone- the Complete Garage Organizer Guide* in 1999. Since then he has written numerous articles about the Great American Garage and has been featured in major newspapers and magazines for his ideas about transforming the garage into functional space. He has appeared on television and been a guest on nationally syndicated radio programs dedicated to home improvement.

He consults with new home builders to establish a 'show garage' in association with model homes. He advises home owners about how to achieve and create a functional garage. Bill also consults with garage remodeling and organizing companies.

He is a member of the National Association of Professional Organizers and a charter member of the Colorado chapter for NAPO.

Bill is a partner and broker associate with The Group, Inc. Real Estate in Fort Collins, Colorado. He has been selling real estate in Northern Colorado since 1977. He earned the Certified Residential Specialist designation in 1981 from the Realtors® National Marketing Institute. Less than 4% of the nation's Realtors® have achieved this designation. He has served on the Colorado Association of Realtors® Executive Committee, and was recognized as the Realtor® of the Year in 1984 by the Fort Collins Board of Realtors®. He served as that organization's president the same year.

He has authored several articles about real estate finance, hazard insurance, and structuring an organization for newcomers in the real estate field that have appeared in national real estate publications.

Bill lives with his wife, Beverly Donnelley M. D., and their son, Taylor, in Fort Collins where he maintains an active real estate practice.

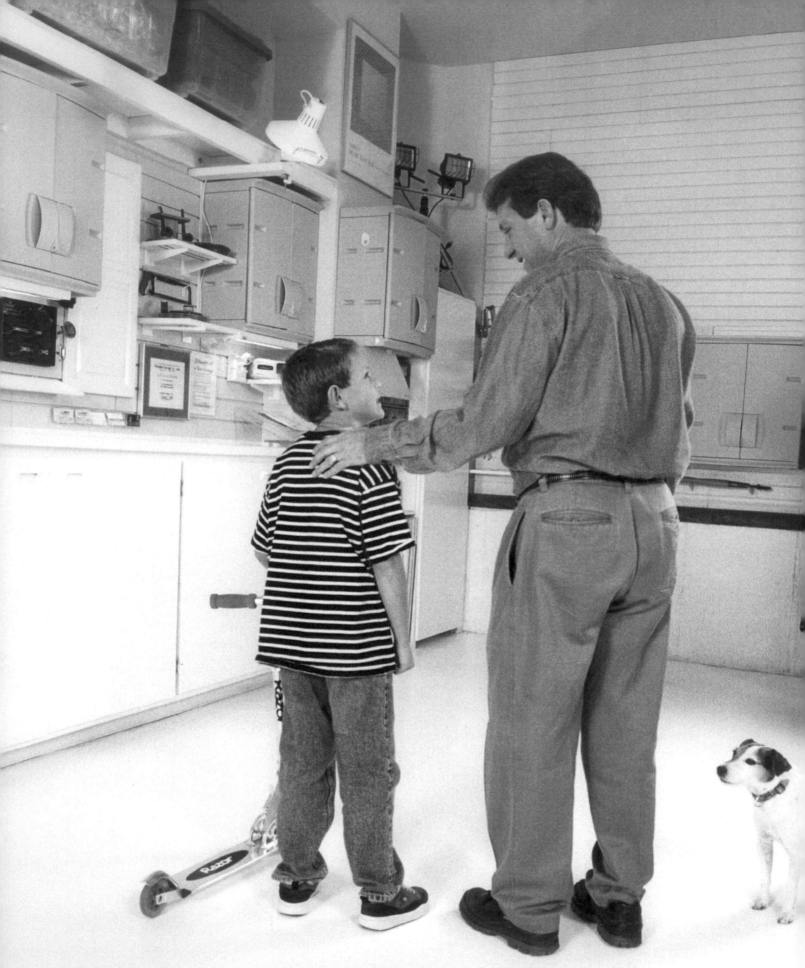

"Just think, son, some day all of this will be yours."